THE KIRKY
OF

TARLAND

Compiled by
SHEILA M SPIERS

ACKNOWLEDGEMENTS

My thanks to Margaret Brown for her initial work here. Before I was on site to start the plan she had the first third of the stones cleaned and read. Thanks also to Mrs Joyce Marchant & Mrs Janet Healey for their work in reading and drawing the plan for the newer section. To Edna Cromarty & Jean Shirer for checking the newer section & to Edna for updating the Index.

1	(Flat) This stone is erected by JOSEPH EMSLIE of Camphill to the memory of JAMES EMSLIE his son d.5 May 1818 aged 3 and his dau. ANN aged 15 d.6 Nov. 1823. Also the foresaid JOSEPH EMSLIE of Camphill d.1 Feb.1849 aged 82. His son ALEXANDER of Camphill d.21 June 1850 aged 40. His wife JEAN LESLIE d.27 May 1851 aged 72. His daus. MARGARET widow of JAMES EMSLIE of Tullochvenus d.16 Apr.1874 aged 58, JEAN of Camphill widow of Rev. JOHN A.MACLENNAN d.3 Dec.1882 aged 83. (Now illegible)

---

2   (Wall) Sacred to the memory of Mrs. JEAN EMSLIE of Camphill, widow of Rev. JOHN AULAY MACLENNAN d.3 Dec.1882 aged 63. 4 lines verse. Erected by her sons.

---

3   Erected in loving memory of ALEXANDER McKIDDIE 2nd son of DAVID McKIDDIE forester d.Tarland Lodge 13 June 1885 aged 32. DAVID eldest son d.19 May 1897 aged 46. ANN SMITH wife of said DAVID McKIDDIE forester d.2 Jan.1898 aged 75, above DAVID McKIDDIE d.30 Sept.1907 in 79th year. Bottom: 1 line text.

---

4   In memory of ADAM SIEVWRIGHT M.R.C.V.S.Tarland, for 44 years vetinary surgeon in this district d.8 Dec.1923 aged 73, his wife BETSY ANDERSON McKIDDIE d.10 July 1941 aged 83. Their dau. ANNIE d.22 Nov.1974 aged 87, their son ALEXANDER McKIDDIE SIEVWRIGHT M.V.O.,M.R.C.V.S. d.15 Jan.1985 aged 86 who practiced as a vetinary surgeon in this district for 43 years. Also their cousin Dr. MILLICENT C.DEWAR of Edinburgh & London 1915 - 1994.

---

6   Erected by JAMES MICHIE in memory of his children who d.at Corrachree: JOHN GAULD 5 July 1885 aged 9mths., and MARGARET FARQUHARSON 12 Oct.1887 aged 9mths. Above JAMES MICHIE d.Whitehouse 22 Apr.1913 aged 65, his wife HELEN MICHIE d.Aberdeen 11 Feb.1930 aged 84. (Shield under) In loving memory of little MAGGIE.

---

6   (Rectangle by wall) HAY - In memory of our loved ones.

---

7   Small white shield - nothing visible.

---

8   In memory of PETER COUTTS d.Backside of Corrachree 12 June 1862 aged 82. His dau. MARY d.Westown 27 Feb.1841 aged 21, his son JOHN d.Backside 20 May 1844 aged 16, his dau. JESSIE d.Dundee 14 Dec.1866 aged 30, his son PETER d.Bellabeg 11 June 1873 aged 38. ANN MACHARDY wife of above PETER COUTTS d.Bargles 19 Dec.1874 aged 78. Bottom: This stone is erected by PETER COUTTS junr.

---

9   Erected by CHARLES COUTTS in memory of his wife MARGARET GLENESK d.Royal Infirmary, Aberdeen 18 May 1893 in 63rd year. Above CHARLES COUTTS d.Pitloine, Logie Coldstone 24 Apr.1894 aged 68.

---

10   (Wall) In memory of ANDREW LAMOND d.31 Mar.1778 aged 73. Also of AGNES MICHIE his wife d.13 Oct.1787 aged 74. (Jervise p.268 adds: 'A broken marble slab shows that the monument was erected in July 1789 by their 2nd son JOHN of Kingston, Jamaica.)

---

11   (Flat) In memory of WILLIAM LAMOND of Stranduff d.13 Feb.1813 aged 72 & ELIZABETH FARQUHARSON his spouse d.30 Nov.1823 aged 80. Also of AGNES their dau. d.21 Feb.1810 aged 27 & JOHN their son who d.in infancy & JAMES LAMOND of Stranduff their eldest son d.9 Jan.1851 aged 70

12	(Flat) In memory of ROBERT DOUGLASS sometime farmer in Meikle Culsh, Tarland d.22 Jan.1841 aged 86 also his spouse ELISABETH LAMOND d.2 Jan.1813 aged 70. Also MARGARET GRANT his 2nd wife d.Mains of Glenbucket 23 Jan.1871 aged 83. Also of their son JAMES LAMOND DOUGLASS sometime farmer at Culsh & Bucham, thereafter bank agent North of Scotland Bank Ltd., Ballater b.6 June 1819 - d.8 Nov.1893.

---

13   In loving memory of ALEXANDER CRAN M.A., M.R.C.S.E. b.Templand, Rhynie 16 Nov. 1803 - d.Wester Clova, Kildrummy 6 Mar.1889. He practised his profession in this parish from 1826 until 1870. He was an elder of the Church of Scotland for 52 years. MARGARET REID his wife b.Templeton, Kildrummy 27 Mar.1811 - d.Wester Clova, Kildrummy 13 Feb. 1890. 3 lines text. (RHS) Also their son ALEXANDER b.3 Apr.1838 - d.Wester Clova, Kildrummy 8 Dec.1883; their dau. MARGARET HARPER b.21 May 1841 - d.10 Apr.1858; ANNE ERSKINE d. Bella-straid 14 Sept.1919 aged 80 & JAMES d.Duncan, Vancouver Island 15 June 1920 aged 71. (Back) Also of their son ROBERT M.D., b.26 Sept.1854 - d.Wemyss Bay 23 Oct.1892. He held medical appointments in Assam for 11 years & after-wards practised in Ballater, the beloved husband of ELISABETH BERTRAM CRAN, only dau. of late JOHN JOHNSTON paper manufacturer Peterculter d.Lochnagar House 30 June 1904 aged 43. (LHS) Their son WILLIAM d.Tarland 26 Feb.1930 aged 79.

---

14   (Flat) Sacred to the memory of WILLIAM NICOL farmer & innkeeper in Stone House, Tarland d.28 Sept.1822 aged 67. Also HELEN DANIEL his 1st wife d.6 Apr.1801 aged 48. This stone was erected by ANN SHIRREFS his 2nd wife.

---

15   Erected in loving memory of ALEXANDER DAWSON crofter Muir of Coynach, Migvie d.4 Oct.1893 aged 77, his wife MARGARET THOMSON d.Coynach 19 Mar.1910 aged 82. Their grandsons DANIEL d.17 Mar.1980 aged 93, JOHN d.11 Feb.1985 aged 99 dear husband of MARGARET CRUICKSHANK d.29 Nov.1981 aged 91.

---

16   Erected by C.WALKER Culsh, Tarland in memory of his sons who d.on active service. Pte. ALLAN M.WALKER killed 20 Sept.1917 aged 20, Gunner CHARLES R.WALKER killed 21 Dec.1917 aged 26. (RHS) Said CHARLES WALKER d.Culsh, Tarland 16 Apr.1925 aged 58, ANNE RIACH his wife d.Lynmore Cottage, Tarland 3 Oct.1934 aged 76. (LHS) ARTHUR STEWART LITTLEJOHN builder d.Lynmore, Tarland 25 May 1952 aged 75, his wife JANE ANNE WALKER d.19 Feb.1966 aged 75. (Back) Also of JAMES W.WALKER late of Culsh, Tarland d.4 May 1965 aged 72, his wife MARGARET ELLIS d.23 Mar.1967 aged 73. Base: Also of their dau. HELEN d.21 Feb.1987 aged 68, wife of AUSTEN HENDERSON d.29 Sept.1987 aged 75. 1 line text.

16a   (Shield) In memory of my aunt ELIZABETH MORRISON d.July 1895 aged 86.

---

17   In memory of MOSES MILNE Drummie, Tarland d.13 Aug.1905 aged 78, his wife ANN McLAREN d.28 Dec.1891 aged 62.

---

18   To the memory of ALEXANDER PROCTOR watchmaker Tarland d.5 May 1859 aged 75, his wife MARGARET MACPHERSON d.20 Apr.1859 aged 68. 2 lines text. Of their family THOMAS d.in infancy 15 Feb.1820, DAVID d.4 Dec.1841 aged 25, ALEXANDER minister of the Gospel Addlington, Berks., England d.10 Nov.1842 aged 30, JOHN surgeon Towie d.4 Apr.1854 aged 44. Base: Erected by the surviving members of their family. (LHS) Sacred to the memory of JAMES PROCTOR b.Tarland 1 Jan.1823 - d.Kirkville House, Skene 31 Jan. 1888 aged 65, his spouse ANN HECTOR b.9 Jan.1823 - d.13 Jan.1913. 5 lines verse. Back:/

| 18 cont. | /Sacred to the memory of MARGARET PROCTOR of Badentoy, only dau. of ALEXANDER PROCTOR & MARGARET MACPHERSON interred here, b.4 May 1828 - d.7 Mar.1915. |

| 19 | Face down. |

| 20 | To the memory of MARGARET M.TAYLOR d.7 Mar.1946 aged 69 wife of ANDREW TAYLOR Barehillock, Tarland. Their son JAMES d.Malaya 19 June 1943 aged 22, their dau. ANNIE d.27 Sept.1945 aged 28. Above ANDREW TAYLOR d.Aberdeen 24 Dec.1959 aged 84. |

| 21 | Erected by ISABELLA ANN SIMPSON in loving memory of her husband ALEXANDER FORBES carpenter d.Gordon Cottage, Tarland 19 Mar.1945 aged 66. Their dau. CATHERINE MITCHELL d.Schoolhill 19 June 1914 aged 9yrs 8mths. Above ISABELLA ANN SIMPSON d.29 Aug.1958 aged 80. |

| 22 | In memory of Rev. JAMES WATSON minister of this parish d.4 Apr.1868 aged 62. Rev. WILLIAM MAITLAND minister of the Gospel in Tarland d.23 Jan.1799 in 67th year of his age & 32nd of his ministry. ELIZABETH McINNES his wife d.21 Feb. 1797. |

| 23 | (Jervise p.268-9 says that the above stone adjoins that of his grandfather, Mr Maitland & quotes a tablestone which is possibly our No.23. We could see nothing.) (Flat) In memory of Rev. WILLIAM MAITLAND minister of the Gospel at Tarland d.23 Jan.1799 in 67th year of his age & 32nd of his ministry. And ELIZABETH McINNES his spouse d.21 Feb.1797. Also of GEORGE their son d.in infancy & ANN their 2nd dau. d.15 Jan.1794 aged 23. Latin motto. |

| 24 | In memory of MARY ROBERTSON wife of JAMES McHARDY d.1 Sept.1877 aged 46, above JAMES McHARDY d.23 Nov.1901 aged 88. CHRISTIANA (sic) CAMERON dau. of above d.12 Jan.1940 aged 86. |

| 25 | In memory of GEORGE EWEN d.California 2 Sept.1886 aged 22, CHARLES EWEN d.1 Oct.1894 aged 20. Their father ROBERT EWEN d.5 Oct.1915 aged 86, his wife JANE ARCHIBALD d.27 May 1919 aged 80. Base: Erected by their brothers. |

| 26 | Erected in memory of DAVID BRUCE farmer North Pett, Tarland d.Aberdeen Royal Infirmary 16 Feb.1927, his wife ELIZABETH MOLLISON d.Burnside, Corrachree, Tarland 28 Feb.1943. |

| 27 | (Marker type) J.S. G.D. |

| 28 | Here lies JOHN TAWES lawfull son to ALEXR. TAWES & MARGARET THOMSON. He d.8 Feb.1781 aged 79. Also CHARLES, GEORGE, WILLIAM, PETER, MARGT. & JEAN TAWES his brothers & sisters. This is done by ISABEL TAWES in memory of her brothers & sisters. |

| 29 | (First part (-) from Jervise) (Here lies the remains of WILLIAM DAVIDSON late farmer in Tarland d.2 day of March 1747 aged about 39 also ELSPET BROWN his spouse who d.in the month of March 1753 aged 46) and JOHN DAVIDSON their eldest son who d.on the fifteenth day of June 17 & seventy three aged thirty years. Done by the care of WILLIAM DAVIDSON their youngest son. |

30   Nothing readable

---

31   (Very little readable on this.)....in Millhead March 1770 of age 59. Also ROBERT WALKER yr. sone who d.Feb....1770 aged 22.

---

32   Here lyes MARJORY ROSS spous to CHARLES HUNTER who dep.this life 2 Mar.1729 & of age 30 years. 8 lines text.

---

33   Here lyes ALLAN McNAB son to the Laird of NcNAB soldier in DUNCAN CAMPBELL's Independent Company who dyed March the 9, 1735 aged 19 years. 5 lines text?

---

34   Erected in memory of JOHN BREBNER Cutishillock d.Dec.1812 aged 56 also of MARGARET WALKER his 1st wife & of MARY WILLIAMS his 2nd wife who d.Nov. 1841. Their children by the 2nd marriage - rest buried. (Back) This memorial of respect for his dear departed relatives is erected by ALEXANDER youngest son living in the State of Illinois, United States, America.

---

35   Erected to the memory of JAMES FORBES late farmer Mains of Kincraigie, Tarland dep.3 June 1855 aged 71 also his dau. ISABELLA FORBES d.24 Dec.1855 aged 31 and ISABELLA HUNTER wife of above JAMES FORBES d.13 Aug.1856 aged 61.

---

36   Erected by JAMES MILNE in memory of his uncle ALEXANDER ESSON d.19 Apr.1886 aged 68. His mother MARY ESSON d.22 Dec.1891 aged 83. His wife ISABELLA REID d.27 June 1893 aged 38. Said JAMES MILNE d.30 Mar.1919 aged 92.

---

37   Erected by ANN FARQUHAR in memory of her husband JOHN CAMERON innkeeper Aberdeen d.30 Oct.1884 aged 69, above ANN FARQUHAR his widow d.Aberdeen 28 Dec. 1906 aged 85. Base: 3 lines text.

---

38   (Book) In loving memory of our mother MARY CRAWFORD MILNE d.12 Mar.1972 aged 89.

---

39   (WG) T4/213251 Driver A.CRAWFORD Royal Army Service Corps 30 Apr.1921 aged 44.

---

40   (Flat) Erected to the memory of CHARLES BEVERLY black-smith in Tarland d.13 Jan. 1836 aged 70. Also his dau. ANN d.21 Aug.1815 aged 7 & his son JEAMS (sic) d.28 Jan 1818 aged 3. Also his wife CATHERINE CRAIB d.6 Mar.1844 aged 68. Also their dau. CATHERINE d.1 Jan.1846 aged 33. Also ALEXANDER BEVERLY d.23 Apr.1853 aged 48, GEORGE d.14 Jan.1883. (No age for George)

---

41   Erected by WILLIAM ALLAN in memory of his wife ELIZABETH ROBERTSON d.28 Jan. 1879 aged 51. Said WILLIAM ALLAN ..... rest of stone gone.

---

42   Face down.

---

43   (In pieces) JOHN STUART son of PETER STUART also farmer in Newmill, Birse d.in 1816 aged 44 leaving a widow & 7 children: MARY d.in 1819, PETER & JOHN in 1846 - all shewing what children are when trained up in the fear of God. His widow, their mother, so truly beloved & respected CHARLOTE (sic) BOYD CATANACH d.18 Jan.1848 aged 72./

| 43 | /ROBERT formerly in Newmill & latterly at Ruthrieston, Old Machar d.15 Apr.1864 aged |
| cont. | 66. MARY ROSS widow of said ROBERT STUART d.11 Oct.1872 aged 78. Bottom: |

43
cont. /ROBERT formerly in Newmill & latterly at Ruthrieston, Old Machar d.15 Apr.1864 aged 66. MARY ROSS widow of said ROBERT STUART d.11 Oct.1872 aged 78. Bottom: Erected by their grateful sons ROBERT farmer in Newmill, HARRY minister Oathlaw, GEORGE schoolmaster of Oathlaw.

----

44 (Flat - In front of the above) PETER STUART farmer in Newmill, Birse was interred here in 1810 in his 84th year of a highly useful religious & respected life. MARY HUNTER his wife in 1818. Also their children WILLIAM, MARY, MARGARET, ANN, HELEN & MICHAL (sic).

----

45 Erected by HARRY & JESSIE STUART in memory of their brother JOHN STUART architect Balgair, Aberdeen d.there 29 Nov.1886 aged 64. Said JESSIE STUART d.there 28 Sept.1901 aged 76.

----

46 In memory of HARRY STUART of Burnside J.P. banker Lumphanan b.15 Jan.1827 - d.2 Oct.1901, his wife ANNE SIVEWRIGHT d.14 Dec.1873. Also their beloved son ROBERT sometime banker Lumphanan b.25 Nov.1853 - d.5 June 1935.

----

47 In loving memory of CATHERINE HARPER wife of JAMES FORBES d.Hill of Boig 27 Apr.1893 aged 48. Above JAMES FORBES d.Gowan Cottage, Tarland 30 Sept.1927 aged 79. Their dau. ISABELLA d.Aberdeen 25 Jan.1962 aged 76.

----

48 In loving memory of JOHN SMITH Ochil Cottage, Tarland d.11 Apr.1909 aged 83, his wife ELLEN WILLIAMSON d.26 Jan.1918. Their daus. CHARLOTTE d.7 Mar.1918, ANNIE GRAHAM MARTIN d.13 Feb.1931. Their granddau. HELEN J.MORGAN B.A.M. d.6 Oct. 1966. Erected by his widow & family. Base: Also their great-granddau. HELEN WINIFRED TOPPING d.17 Apr.1981. (Plaque) Also their great-grandson JOHN SMITH MORGAN d.19 Oct.1992 (No age given)

----

49 In memory of GEORGE BAIN tailor & clothier Tarland d.8 May 1925 aged 58. Of his sons ANDREW d.in infancy 4 July 1891, WILLIAM ALEXANDER d.12 Dec.1908 aged 14. JANE CALDER wife of above GEORGE BAIN d.18 Aug.1943 aged 79. Their daus. GEORGINA CALDER NAPIER d.in July 1968 aged 78, JEAN ANN LEGGE d.3 Dec. 1986 aged 94. Their grand-dau. JEAN NAPIER 1929 - 2000.

----

50 Sacred to the memory of JANE ROSS wife of Rev. WILLIAM SKINNER minister of this parish b.21 Feb.1839 - d.19 Oct.1875. Their infant son JAMES FORBES b.13 July 1868 - d.11 July 1869. Rev. WILLIAM SKINNER b.22 May 1830 - d.30 Dec. 1912 for 44 years minister of this parish. 1 line text. MARGARET ISABELLA MACPHERSON his 2nd wife b.11 Apr.1837 - d.18 Jan.1925.

----

51 In loving memory of JAMES SKINNER son of JAMES SHEPHERD Johannesburg b.21 Sept.1892 - d.12 June 1900. (Now broken)

----

52 In memory of MICHAEL ROY Rowan Bank, Tarland d.26 July 1984 aged 86 & of MARY ISABELLA ROY his younger dau. d.there 3 July 1898. ANN DUNN ROY his elder dau. d.Aberdeen 9 June 1907.

----

53 (Heart) 1881 ISABELLA A.BEY aged 15, ANNIE BEY aged 13.

----

54 Sacred to the memory of JAMES SMITH tenant of the farm of Knowes, Finzean, Birse for 41 years d.6 Mar.1887 aged 69. His brothers JOHN d.there 31 May 1901 aged 74, WILLIAM d.Bridgend, Leochel 27 May 1902 aged 71.

----

55 In memory of ELIZABETH dau.of ALEXANDER SMITH Bridgend, Leochel d.30 July 1869 aged 1. His sons ALEXANDER d.28 Jan.1889 aged 18, JAMES d.26 Jan.1892 aged 18 (LHS) WILLIAM SMITH d.29 Aug.1896 aged 28. Said ALEXANDER SMITH Bridgend, Leochel d.10 Sept.1900 aged 72, his wife ELIZABETH HALL d.there 2 Oct.1902 aged 56.

----

56 In memory of JOHN HUNTER Oldtown of Kincraigie d.10 Mar.1895 aged 74, his wife HELEN ALEXANDER d.there 1 May 1918 aged 83.

----

57 (Flat) This stone is erected in memory of CHARLES FERRES who lived some time in Mickl Corry in Cromar. He d.at Aberdeen 18 Oct.1771 aged 63 & of MARGARET RITCHIE his spouse d.Jwn 5 1776 aged 67. (Spellings as on stone)

----

58 1875. To the memory of PETER FERRES Mill of Culsh d.25 Mar.1875 aged 59, his dau. CHRISTINA d.23 Apr.1876 aged 17. Base: His wife ISABELLA MACANDREW d.2 Aug. 1896 aged 74. (RHS) 1880. To the memory of GEORGE FERRES Mill of Culsh d.8 Nov. 1880 aged 61. (LHS) 1905. To the memory of WILLIAM FERRES farmer Hillhead of Kintocher, Lumphanan d.1 June 1905 aged 42. (Back) Also JANE dau. of PETER FERRES d.Allancriech, Ballogie 30 Dec.1947 aged 82.

----

59 Sacred to the memory of ALEXANDER McROBBIE d.Drumlassie, Kincardine O'Neil 30 May 1870 aged 66, his spouse ELIZABETH DUNCAN d.7 Dec.1883 aged 78.

----

60 In loving memory of my husband DAVID ESSON Aultonrea, Glenmuick, Ballater d.24 Apr. 1945 aged 86. His wife ANN BROWN d.27 Jan.1972 aged 96. Bottom: Erected by his widow & family.

----

61 Erected by JAMES ESSON Burnhead, Lumphanan in memory of his spouse ISABEL LAING d.3 July 1861 aged 63. Said JAMES ESSON d.there 29 May 1866 aged 69.

----

62 (Marker type) C.E.

----

63 (Cross - now face down) In memory of ROBERT ESSON farmer Tillyhermick d.22 Apr. 1932 aged 80.

----

64 (Flat - left & right edges gone) Erected by CHRISTIAN ANDERSON in memory of her husband (ALEX)ANDER ANDERSON/ (fa)rmer in Millhead..../this life 26 June 1832 aged 66/ (Al)so of their son (ALE)XANDER ANDERSON/...Millhead 30 Apr.1854 aged 78.

----

65 Erected by HELEN ANDERSON in memory of her husband JOHN ESSON late farmer in Waulkmill d.28 Jan.1853 aged 63, said HELEN ANDERSON his spouse d.there 23 July 1865 aged 82. ROBERT ESSON son of above d.2 Jan.1879 aged 62, his wife MARGARET CROMAR d.21 July 1894 aged 64. HARRIET McCOMBIE wife of JOHN ESSON d.18 July 1900. MARGARET RIACH 2nd wife of JOHN ESSON d.5 Feb.1935. JOHN ESSON d.22 Feb.1937 at Waulkmill, Tarland.

----

66 In loving memory of ISABELLA PAUL BARRACK or ESSON d.Montrose 30 Apr.1902 aged 72. This stone is erected by her husband Rev. ALEXANDER ESSON late headmaster of Birse Public School, whose parents & other relatives are also interred near this same spot. Said Rev. ALEXANDER ESSON d.Aberdeen 4 Jan.1906 aged 80. MARY ANN their dau. d.there 19 Dec.1927 aged 63.

----

67 In memory of ISABEL ESSON spouse of the late JOHN MICHIE farmer in Broomhill d.17 Apr.1838.

----

68 In memory of HENRY ESSON farmer Balnacraig, Aboyne d.19 Oct.1874 aged 53. His dau. CATHERINE d.22 July 1874 aged 10. His widow ELSPET GRANT d.Auchintarf, Aboyne 23 Apr.1911 aged 80. Bottom: Erected by his widow.

----

69 In memory of ROBERT ESSON farmer Balnacraig, Aboyne d.18 Jan.1851 aged 73, MARY FORBES his wife d.Boghead, Aboyne 17 Apr.1875 aged 85. Of their family CATHERINE aged 36, JANE aged 11, HENRY aged 53, MARGARET aged 20 & ROBERT aged 3.

----

70 (Flat) Here lies the remains of MARGARET ROSS lawful dau. to JAMES ROSS some time farmer in Bogstown & also lawful spouse to ROBERT EASSON (sic) farmer in Milnhead d.July the 6 1791 aged 63/8? 4 lines verse. Also their son ROBERT ESSON sometime farmer in Belna Craig (sic) d.1 Aug.1850 aged 78, & his spouse JANE REID d.18 June 1852 aged 80.

----

71 (Flat) In memory of MARGARET LUMSDEN spouse to WILLIAM ESSON farmer in Melgum d.5 Sept.1821 aged 37. Also hir (sic) son GEORGE d.5 May 1823 aged 11 & 3 of their children who d.in infancy. The above named WILLIAM......at Melgum 21 Feb.1880 aged 7-. (Stone badly broken at bottom)

----

72 In loving memory of our parents ROBERT BIRSS d.17 Sept.1874 aged 84 & HELEN ESSON d.6 Nov.1876 aged 88.

----

73 Erected in memory of our mother ANNE BIRSS or MASSON d.Stonehaven 19 Mar.1913 aged 90 & widow of CHARLES MASSON d.Kirkwall 8 July 1859 aged 34 & was interred there. HELEN BIRSS MacKAY dau. of above d.26 Mar.1942 aged 87, for many years resident in Stonehaven - sadly missed by her family.

----

74 In memory of JAMES BEGG late in Westerton, Migvie d.in June 1821 aged 63. Also his spouse ELSPET OGG d.Mar.1838 aged 90 also 2 of their children BARBARA & JOHN d.in infancy. Ther (sic) 3rd dau. DOROTHY d.20 July 1851 aged 58.

----

75 In memory of JACK G.COUTTS 1925 - 1982, b.at Smallburn, Tarland.

----

76 In loving memory of ETHEL BEVERIDGE d.27 Mar.1927 aged 23, wife of JOHN A. COUTTS d.13 Apr.1985 aged 86. Also their son FRANK d.22 Feb.1990 beloved husband of JEAN WATSON.

----

77 In loving memory of Cpl. ROBERT BAPTIE 8th Gordon Hghrs., son of ROBERT & MARY BAPTIE d.Muirton, Tarland 28 Aug.1916 aged 22, MARY BOOKLESS mother of above & wife of ROBERT BAPTIE d.Muirton 3 Oct.1926 aged 71, ROBERT BAPTIE d.Tarland 29 Mar.1934 aged 79.

78   In loving memory of THOMAS BOOKLESS d.The Muirton, Tarland 28 Nov.1921 aged 70
        Bottom: Erected by his son & dau. ARCHIBALD & MARION.

In loving memory of GEORGE STEWART J.P.d.24 July 1940 aged 68, husband of JANET
LIGHTBODY. Their family: COLIN d.in infancy, ALEXANDER d.27 Sept.1915 aged 19,
79   GORDON d.28 Sept.1915 aged 18, JOHN d.17 Oct.1915 aged 20 - all 3 fell in action in the
Great War. MABEL d.9 Jan.1927 aged 21. Above JANET LIGHTBODY d.28 Nov.1950 aged
79. Their eldest dau. EDITH YOUNG d.17 May 1977, interred at St.Moluags Churchyard.
HILDA youngest child of above Mr & Mrs GEORGE STEWART d.15 July 1995.

In loving memory of GEORGE INNES bootmaker Tarland b.3 May 1827 - d.12 Aug.1905,
his wife MARGARET McRAE b.3 May 1829 - d.9 July 1920. Their son GEORGE d.11
80   Sept.1926 aged 70, their dau. MARGARET d.26 Feb.1951 aged 88. (LHS) Also of RHODA
JOYCE BROCK wife of ALEXANDER INNES b.26 Nov.1872 - d.4 June 1914. Above
ALEXANDER INNES bootmaker Tarland d.8 July 1936 aged 68.

In loving memory of JOHN MACLEAN Tarland d.there 2 Nov.1863 aged 49, MARGARET
FORBES his wife d.Bellastraid, Dinnet 19 May 1889 aged 67. Their only son JOHN R.
81   MACLEAN M.A., b.15 Feb.1859 - d.9 May 1903 at Johannesburg, S.Africa. (LHS) Their
daus. ISABELLA d.3 Mar.1928, ANNIE b.13 July 1847 - d.Oldmeldrum 16 Dec.1940. (RHS)
Their daus. ALEXANDRA ALICE b.21 July 1864 - d.25 Jan.1893, LIZZIE d.14 July 1912,
MARY d.Northampton, in Mar.1919.

----

82   In memory of JAMES FORBES late of Sydney, Australia d.28 Feb.1939 aged 82.

In memory of JOHN FORBES farmer Mureton (sic) d.13 Nov.1893 aged 70, his wife
CHARLOTTE MARY FARQUHARSON CLARK d.21 Aug.1916 aged 90. Their family:
83   MARGARET d.26 Oct.1908 aged 49, ANNIE d.6 Apr.1909 aged 48, ELIZABETH d.25
Feb.1911 aged 54, ISABELLA d.28 Oct.1936 aged 75 & MARY d.30 July 1956 aged 90.

----

84   In affectionate remembrance of JANET FORBES d.13 Apr.1911 aged 21.

Erected by ALEXANDER FORBES flesher Tarland in memory of his wife MARGARET
McALLAN d.22 Dec.1899 aged 68. Their dau. HARRIET d.in infancy, their 2nd son
85   MAXWELL d.24 Apr.1902 aged 38. Above ALEXANDER FORBES d.18 Dec.1905 aged
80. Their daus. ISABELLA d.4 July 1934 aged 69, JEAN MORRICE d.27 Feb.1946 aged
77.

----

86   In loving memory of JAMES E.SMITH d.3 Apr.1964. His wife LILY PETERS d.14 May
1987, late of Culsh, Bridge of Gairn.

86a   In loving memory of MARY & REBECCA STUART, JAMES F.STUART, ROBERT
W.A.STUART, JAMES D.S.STUART.

----

87   In loving memory of CHARLES GILL d.Blelack, Dinnet 19 Mar.1964 aged 90 husband of
MARGARET CHEYNE d.Insch 26 Oct.1985 aged 80.

In memory of CHARLES GRASSICK farmer Tarland d.20 Nov.1884 aged 93, his wife JANE
88   CALDER d.23 May 1861 aged 63. Their dau. REBECCA d.in Apr.1861 aged 36, their son
ALEXANDER d.17 July 1869 aged 48. Their daus. JANE d.30 June 1896 aged 69,/

88 cont.	/ELIZABETH d.2 June 1900 aged 72. Their son CHARLES d.25 Dec.1913 aged 72, their dau. MARY d.25 Apr.1919 aged 72.

89	(Flat - Top rim) This stone & inscription was restored in 1902. Here lys JOHN DAVIDSON who was born in the beginning of the present century, lived all his life time in Tarland & died there on the third of March 1787 going 82 years of age; with 2 of his children JAMES & JEAN DAVIDSONS who died in their infancy. This being the burial place of their family for several centurys (sic), where many of them are interred since the first of whom, a captain, was settled in this country by the IRVINES of Drum, for a particular favour he had done that family at Edinburgh, in the time of the Stewart, or Scottish kings. Done by the care of MARGARET McCOMBE, the defunct's relict, her eldest son JOHN DAVIDSON of Tillychetly & his dau. ANN DAVIDSON in Tarland. His 2nd son CHARLES DAVIDSON d.in Jamaica some time ago. 2 lines verse. (See also Kincardine O'Neil No.304)

90	(Flat) Here lie the remains of JOHN GAULD sometime farmer in Westtown d.22 July 1759 aged 47 leaving behind 3 children JOHN, HARY & JEAN GAULDS. Also BARBARA INGRAM his spouse d.9 June 1822 in the advanced age of 89 years. Also their son JOHN d.7 Dec.1841 in the 77? year of his age. And HARRY GAULD d.27? Mar.1848 aged 29, also HARRY GAULD his father d.24 July 1856? aged 77 & his wife MARGARET OGG d.25 Aug.1861 aged 80. Done by the care of ELISABETH GAULD their dau. Bottom: This stone is placed here by the filial affection of his 2 sons.

91	In memory of JOHN GAULD late farmer Nether Corrachree d.7 Mar.1868 aged 56, his son PETER d.6 July 1851 aged 10. His dau. BARBRA d.in infancy. His wife ELIZABETH RITCHIE d.9 Mar.1891 aged 79. Bottom: Erected by his sons JOHN & ROBERT.

92	In loving memory of CATHERINE ANGUS FORBES wife of JOHN MITCHELL d.Ennets, Tornaveen 3 Nov.1935 aged 64. Above JOHN MITCHELL d.Forresterhill 26 Nov.1942 aged 75. Their dau. GRACE ISABELLA d.Cairndaie Croft, Sauchen 12 Sept.1958 aged 51. (Now face down)

93	In loving memory of JOHN EWEN late farmer Downside, Tarland d.Westtown 4 June 1889 aged 82.

94	In memory of ROBERT EWEN wright in Bogg d.22 Nov.1785 aged 59. His spouse ELSPET SECKTER d.6 Mar.1812 aged 85. Their son JOHN late farmer in West-town d.17 June 1818 aged 58. By their son ROBERT & grandson JOHN.

95	In loving memory of Pte. GEORGE MUNRO 7th Gordon Hlrs., T.F.who was killed by shrapnel & buried near Festubert 26 May 1915 aged 18. His sister BELLA d.suddenly at Tarland Lodge 17 Sept.1915 aged 22. Their mother HELEN REID d.Gateside Cottage, Strachan 18 Feb.1935 aged 74, also their father (not named) d.22 Feb.1938 aged 73. Bottom: Erected by parents & family, Tarland Lodge.

96	Erected by ALEXANDER FRAIN in memory of his wife ANN McANDREW d.5 May 1867 aged 40. Of their family JAMES d.27 Feb.1866 aged 1, ALEXANDER d.11 Apr.1867 aged 4, JOHN d.4 May in infancy, WILLIAM d.19 May 1867 aged 8. Above ALEXANDER FRAIN d.27 Dec.1906 aged 86. (Space) And of his father WILLIAM d.24 May 1866 aged 72, ELISABETH MIDDLETON his wife d.15 Feb.1884 aged 93.

---

97 In loving memory of MARY MORRISON STEWART wife of JAMES COUTTS d.15 Oct. 1963 aged 77. Above JAMES COUTTS retired farmer late of Rothiemay, Tarland d.23 Mar. 1966 aged 83.

----

98 Sacred to the memory of JAMES THOMPSON FORBES b.23 Dec.1887 - d.10 Mar.1897 son of JAMES FORBES teacher Tarland. And of JAMES FORBES M.A., 41 years school-master of this parish b.9 May 1855 - d.17 Sept.1922. His widow ELIZABETH FRASER THOMPSON d.17 June 1944 in 83rd year. (Plaque below) JAMES T.FORBES. Placed here by his schoolmates 1897.

----

99 In memory of ALEXANDER BEY d.23 June 1920 aged 56, his wife MARGARET TROUP d.6 Jan.1937 aged 65. Their family JAMES d.13 June 1913 aged 13, CATHERINE d.28 Oct. 1899 aged 4.

----

100 (This stone is badly worn on the right side & a piece is missing from the left side.) Here lyes WILLIAM SIMPSON tennant? at Mill of Tarland? who dyed 11 Nov? 1742 aged 63? his daus. ISSOBEL aged 22, MARY aged 22, ELSPET aged 21? Done by the care of JOHN SIMPSON his oldest son.

----

101 Erected by JAMES BREBNER in memory of his father & mother JOHN BREBNER & ANN SMITH also his brothers & sisters & his wife ANNE GLASS d.2 Apr.1860 aged 30. Above JAMES BREBNER d.Aberdeen 29 June 1907 aged 74. His dau. MARY ANNIE BREBNER or SELWAY d.there 6 Feb.1929 aged 73, widow of WILLIAM SELWAY Edinburgh.

----

102 In loving memory of JOHN McARTHUR d.12 Dec.1965 aged 85 husband of AGNES McDONALD. Their dau. AGNES d.in infancy. Above AGNES McDONALD d.19 June 1980 aged 95. (Heart) In loving memory of AGNES McARTHUR.

----

103 Erected by ALEXANDER McROBERT woollen manufacturer Cawnpore, British India in loving memory of his parents JOHN McROBERT farmer Douneside in this parish d. there 21 Aug.1904 aged 78. HELEN COLLIE or McROBERT d.Douneside aforesaid 6 July 1906 aged 73. Base: 2 lines text.

----

104 Sacred to the ever abiding memory of ALEXANDER McROBERT ANDERSON dearly beloved child of WILLIAM & MAGGIE ANDERSON Home Farm, Hopewell, Tarland b.17 June 1907 - d.by accident 23 Nov.1910. 2 lines verse.

----

105 In memory of JOHN TAWSE farmer Strathweltie b.6 Mar.1791 - d.10 Apr.1860. WILLIAM TAWSE b.17 June 1793 - d.14 Feb.1873. JAMES TAWSE b.5 Mar.1798 - d.27 May 1880. Their sister MARGARET TAWSE b.13 Sept.1800 - d.3 June 1881. Bottom: Erected by GEORGE TAWSE.

----

106 Erected by JAMES TAWSE farmer in Neuk, Logie Coldstone in memory of his father JOHN TAWSE d.there 8 Dec.1842 aged 75, his mother JEAN SMITH or TAWSE d.6 Aug 1861 aged 83. His brothers CHARLES aged 18, ALEXANDER aged 4mths., ALEXANDER aged 13mths.,GEORGE medical student aged 23. Of his sisters ANN d.31 Dec.1879 aged 73, ISABELLA TAWSE or ILLINGWORTH d.19 Sept.1884 aged 84. Said JAMES TAWSE d.at Neuk 20 Sept.1888 aged 72.

----

107 In memory of ELIZABETH SMITH wife of CHARLES BREBNER Tarland d.15 Jan.1865 aged 57. Their children CHARLES & JANE d.in infancy. Said CHARLES BREBNER d.13 Apr.1893 aged 84. Their son JOHN d.Tarland 9 July 1908 aged 65, their dau. ISABELLA d.13 Jan.1916 aged 64. Her husband PATRICK REID watchmaker & jeweller Tarland d.29 Dec.1937 aged 85. Their daus. ELIZABETH REID d.28 Feb.1911 aged 20, MARY A.REID or GLENISTER d.7 Oct.1944 aged 58, her husband WILLIAM G.GLENISTER M.Inst.C.E., d.26 Mar.1940 - interred High Wycombe. Base: Their son CHARLES BREBNER REID watchmaker & jeweller d.18 Apr.1951 aged 64, his wife MARGARET MILNE d.27 Dec. 1969 aged 77.

---

108 Erected by WILLIAM BREBNER contractor at Coull in memory of his wife CATHERINE GORDON d.26 Nov.1850 aged 43. Their dau. ANN d.in infancy, ISABELLA d.Woolwich 17 May 1891 aged 47, JOHN d.Ballater 30 Oct.1892 aged 46. Above WILLIAM BREBNER d.Knowhead 20 Apr.1899 aged 86, his 2nd wife MARGARET ADAM d.Aboyne 15 Aug. 1915 aged 94. Their dau. MARY widow of Dr. FORBES d.5 July 1915 aged 56.

---

109 Erected in affectionate remembrance of ISOBEL SIMPSON wife of CHARLES BREBNER Drummie, Tarland d.28 July 1864 aged 70 & is buried here. Of the following 4 of their children who d.unmarried: MARY d.June 1836 aged 11, CHARLES d.July 1836 aged 15, BETSY d.Aug.1860 aged 41 - all of whom are buried in this churchyard. Rev. ROBERT BREBNER d.Ashbourne, Derbyshire 22 Jan.1859 aged 26 & is interred at Osmaston in the same county. Above CHARLES BREBNER d.17 Oct.1876 aged 81 & is also buried here.

---

110 (Small Shield) Mother 5 Sept.1915.

---

111 Erected by GEORGE NIVEN in memory of his children GEORGE & JOHN d.in infancy, ALEXANDER d.3 Feb.1847 aged 17 also of his wife ELISABETH WALKER d.3 Sept.1849 aged 46. Their daus. ISABELLA d.24 July 1859 aged 13, ELISABETH d.13 Aug.1859 aged 18 of diphtheria. The above GEORGE NIVEN d.18 Feb.1876 aged 78, his dau. MARY WALKER NIVEN d.15 Mar.1919 aged 84.

---

112 1868. Erected by JOHN NIVEN Knowhead, Lumphannan (sic) in memory of his dau. MARGARET d.10 June 1868 in 48th year, his wife JANE GORDON d.27 June 1868 aged 81. Above JOHN NIVEN d.Oldyleaper, Birse 14 June 1879 aged 86.

---

113 Erected by JOHN NEVEN (sic) Oldyleeper, Birse in memory of his dau. MARY d.22 June 1876 aged 10. JOHN NIVEN d.16 Mar.1900 aged 73, his wife ELSPET ROBERTSON d.Torphins 6 Sept.1918 aged 77. Their son JOHN d.11 Feb.1929 aged 63, their dau. MAGGIE ANN d.Banchory 25 June 1930 aged 44.

---

114 In fond memory of MARGARET FORBES dau. of ALEXANDER & ANNIE HOWIE d.21 May 1919 aged 1 year 10 mths.

---

115 In loving memory of MARGARET FORBES wife of JAMES GARIOCH d.Newton, Logie Coldstone 21 Jan.1941 aged 70, above JAMES GARIOCH d.Tillylodge, Lumphanan 2 Aug. 1944 aged 74. ANNIE BARBARA GARIOCH wife of ALEX.HOWIE jun. Schoolhouse, Coull d.22 May 1922 aged 26. MARTHA STRACHAN GARIOCH Inver Hotel, Crathie d.12 Aug.1970 aged 71, MAY GARIOCH or WARREN d.2 Mar.1972 - daus. of JAMES & MARGARET GARIOCH.

---

116   In loving memory of my husband ALEXANDER GRANT d.17 Apr.1921.

---

117   In memory of JAMES HUNTER FERRIES husband of ISABELLA ARCHIE d.Cotmore 3 Jan.1938 aged 74. Their family: ANNIE d.31 May 1920 aged 37, JAMES HUNTER fell in action 28 Mar.1918 aged 22. Above ISABELLA ARCHIE d.Cotmore 17 May 1955 aged 93. (Now lying on its back)

---

118   In memory of ELIZABETH REID d.Tarland 1 July 1917 aged 86. PETER REID Crathie father of above, served his country as a soldier in the Peninsular War & at Waterloo.

---

119   (WG) 290098 Pte. A.W.CRUICKSHANK Gordon Hlrs. 7 Nov.1918 aged 39.

---

120   (Heart) FORREST. In loving memory of my dear husband.

---

121   In loving memory of JIM & Daddy. SMITH.

---

122   In memory of ROBERT TAYLOR Wester Knowhead d.7 Mar.1834 aged 62, MARGERET (sic) DAVIDSON his wife d.9 Dec.1878 aged 83. Their sons JAMES d.31 Mar.1848 aged 23, ROBERT d.3 Feb.1900 aged 77. His family: ROBERT d.in infancy, JAMES aged 2, MARY aged 17, WILLIAM aged 36. His wife MARY ANN STEWART aged 69. JOHN TAYLOR d.4 Apr.1962. ELIZABETH TAYLOR d.6 May 1964, her husband JAMES A. TAYLOR d.26 Feb.1972.

---

123   (Marker type) M.O. 1810. (Plaque in front) MARY TAYLOR aged 17.

---

124   In loving memory of ANNIE GORDON FINDLAY wife of ROBERT TAYLOR Jun.d.Wester Knowhead 10 June 1930 aged 70, above ROBERT TAYLOR d.Greenmoss, Kemnay 15 Oct. 1934 aged 87. Also their daus. NELLIE d.11 Sept.1962, ROBINA d.22 Jan.1974.

---

125   Erected by ISABELLA MILNE in memory of her husband JAMES MILNE mason d.Tarland 31 May 1897 aged 85, above ISABELLA MILNE d.23 Oct.1902 aged 89

---

126   1903. Erected to the memory of ALEXANDER McCONNACH late postman Tarland d.21 Oct.1901 aged 77, his son JAMES d.8 July 1874 aged 5, his daus. ELSIE d.17 June 1881 aged 9, JANE d.Tarland 21 June 1904 aged 35. His wife ELIZABETH THOMSON d.17 Feb. 1915 aged 80.

---

127   Erected by JAMES McCONNACH in memory of his wife ANN THOMSON d.1 Dec.1842 aged 41. Above JAMES McCONNACH d.29 Mar.1890 aged 88. Their son LEWIS d.24 Jan. 1877 aged 43, their dau. ANNIE d.11 Apr.1903 aged 76.

---

128   In loving memory of ISABELLA COUTTS d.6 Mar.1946 aged 57. Her husband ALEXANDER CUMMING d.15 Nov.1966 aged 88.

---

129   In loving memory of ROBERT McALLAN late farmer Whiteley, Tarland d.12 June 1963 aged 68, youngest son of late GEORGE & MARGARET McALLAN, Mill of Kincraigie, Tarland. His sister MAGGIE ANN McALLAN d.24 May 1977 aged 85.

---

130   In loving remembrance of MARGARET ANN CRAIK wife of WILLIAM BROWN miller Tarland d.20 Dec.1908 aged 55, their twin sons GEORGE & JAMES d.in infancy. Their son/

| 130 cont. | /CHARLES d.11 Dec.1920 aged 38. Above WILLIAM BROWN d.9 Apr.1921 aged 68, their son JOHN d.11 Oct.1943 aged 64. |

---

131   In loving memory of our father ALEXANDER GRANT d.19 Jan.1880 aged 41, our sister BARBARA HELEN d.15 Oct.1891 aged 22. Our mother ELIZABETH REID d.22 Jan.1938 aged 89.

---

132   In memory of PETER GRANT late merchant in Tarland d.10 May 1842 aged 44 & 4 of their children who d.in infancy. Their son ALEXANDER GRANT d.19 Jan.1880 aged 44. HELEN SKEEN their mother d.11 Mar.1883 aged 83.

---

133   In cherished memory of JAMES HUNTER SHEPHERD Aberdeen Arms Hotel, Tarland d.28 Mar.1963 aged 52, dear husband of ISOBEL SCOTT d.16 Sept.1989 aged 77.

---

134   In memory of CHARLES SKENE farmer Whitelay d.1854. ISOBELLA HENDERSON his wife d.1842. Their sons CHARLES d.1845, JOHN d.1853.

---

135   (Flat) Sacred to the memory of JOHN SKENE late merchant in Tarland d.14 July 1817 aged 32? Also of ISABEL, JOHN, JOHN & ANN his children who d.young. CHARLES d.10 Feb. 1825 aged 14. Also his spouse ANN LITTLEJOHN d.12 Nov.1836? aged 51. Also LEWIS their last surviving son d.23 May 1839 aged 23.

---

136   Erected by ROBERT & BARBARA McCONNACHIE Braeside, Slack, Tarland in loving memory of their children: BARBARA d.24 Apr.1905 aged 7, JOHN, ROBERT, ROBINA & CATHERINE d.in infancy, ADAM d.5 Oct.1920 aged 20. Above BARBARA McCONNACHIE d.Hillock, Tarland 14 Oct.1943 aged 71, above ROBERT McCONNACHIE d.Braeside, Slack, Tarland 30 Dec.1952 aged 75.

---

137   In loving memory of JAMES CLARK farmer Upper Watererne d.18 Mar.1901 aged 71, his wife MARGARET FYFE d.20 Jan.1907 aged 79. Their grandson ALEXANDER SMITH d.30 Apr.1936 aged 44, their dau. ANNIE CLARK d.30 Mar.1952 aged 82.

---

138   Erected by the surviving family in memory of their father & mother WILLIAM CLARK late of Waterside, Ferrar, Aboyne d.Deecastle 23 July 1860 aged 62, his wife BETTY DUNCAN d.16 Sept.1877 aged 79. Their sons ALEXANDER d.6 Dec.1839 aged 18, WILLIAM d.Daisy Cottage, Torphins 23 Apr.1903 in 76th year. Their dau. MARGARET d.East Roseburn, Aboyne 6 Mar.1917 in 93rd year.

---

139   (Shield) In memory of JOHN COOPER aged 64.

---

140   In memory of JAMES WALKER d.Parkside of Corrachree 4 Apr.1887 aged 69, his wife ANN FARQUHAR d.Woodside of Corrachree 19 Dec.1900 aged 81. Bottom. Erected by his widow.

---

141   In memory of JAMES CLARK d.Burnside of Correchree (sic) 28 Mar.1866 aged 71, his wife MARGRET SMITH d.there 13 Apr.1880 aged 87.

---

142   Erected by CHARLES & MARIA WILSON CLARK in loving memory of their dau. MAGGIE d.Burnside, Corrachree 13 Nov.1901 aged 13. Above CHARLES CLARK d.Cedar Bank, Tarland 8 Jan.1921 aged 85, MARIA WILSON GLASS wife of above d.there 14 July/

142cont./1932 aged 78. Their dau. ANNIE d.16 Feb.1964 aged 80.

143
Erected by his widow & family in loving remembrance of WILLIAM SIMPSON d.St. Margarets, Correchree 28 Apr.1901 aged 72, for 36 years Police Constable & 8 years Inspector of Poor, Tarland. His children JANE d.Tulloch, Strathdon 26 Jan 1877 aged 10, LIZZIE d.Calsie, Clatt 8 Sept.1891 aged 20. His widow ELIZABETH CLARK d.St.Margarets 28 June 1910 aged 80.

144
In memory of WILLIAM CLARK farmer Mains of Hopewell d.26 Apr.1912 aged 88, his wife JEAN KESSON d.3 June 1914 aged 84. Their sons WILLIAM d.14 Oct.1869 aged 8, JOHN d.in infancy.

145
In affectionate remembrance of JANET McKENZIE wife of JAMES S.CLARK d.Mains of Hopewell, Tarland 17 Nov.1930 aged 57, above JAMES CLARK d.4 Woodend Place, Aberdeen 21 Dec.1944 aged 77. Their dau. JANE ANN CLARK d.4 Jan.1983 aged 85.

146
In loving memory of MARY ANN MILNE d.Church Square, Ballater 11 Jan.1898 aged 53. Her mother MARGARET FALCONER d.Drochet, Ballater 9 Jan.1903 aged 79. Bottom: 2 lines text.

147
Sacred to the memory of DUNCAN SMITH late blacksmith in Coatmore d.27 Oct.1833 aged 41, also GEORGE his son d.in infancy, also of his spouse HELEN WEBSTER d.5 Nov.1840 aged 49. (Now broken against the wall)

148
In memory of WILLIAM SMITH Inland Revenue officer Tomatin, Inverness d.26 Nov.1903 aged 44, his wife MARGARET ANN McKENZIE d.12 Dec.1903 aged 35. Their youngest son Pte. MALCOLM NORMAN 6th Gordon Hlrs., was killed in action in France 13 Oct. 1918 aged 19.

---

149   In memory of WILLIAM SMITH carpenter d.Glack, Migvie 24 Aug.1894 aged 63.

150
In loving memory of JAMES JEFFREY farmer Meadow, Migvie d.13 Jan.1907 aged 53, his wife ANNIE SMITH d.28 Dec.1945 aged 82 - interred Frankby, Cheshire.

151
Erected by ALEXANDER BRUCE COPLAND in memory of his wife ANNIE INGRAM d.Easter Daugh, Tarland 8 Oct.1913 aged 60. Above ALEXANDER BRUCE COPLAND d.2 Jan 1938 aged 84. Their dau. ELIZABETH MARY d.Ailsa, Tarland 12 Mar.1960 aged 70.

152
(Face mostly gone) ...memory of/....(CHAR)LES REID/....farmer in West-town../ Aug.1822 aged 86, his spouse ISABELLA MUIL?.....

---

153   (Marker type) A.G. M.G. 1812.

154
(Shield) In loving memory of ADAM GEORGE d.12 May 1935, his brother ALEXANDER d.18 May 1935. Erected by his widow.

155
Erected by WILLIAM GEORGE Crossfold in loving memory of his sons WILLIAM d.6 Mar. 1876 aged 1, ADAM d.16 July 1904 aged 27. His dau. WILHEMINA (sic) d.14 Sept.1905 aged 45, MARY d.4 July 1907 aged 34. (LHS) FREDERICK W.d.19 Apr. 1920 aged 61, ANN d.15 Aug.1920 aged 40. His wife ANN ADAMS d.17 Mar.1928 aged 87, said/

| 155 cont. | /WILLIAM GEORGE d.26 Sept.1928 aged 93. (Heart under) In memory of ADAM GEORGE aged 27. |

155
cont.   /WILLIAM GEORGE d.26 Sept.1928 aged 93. (Heart under) In memory of ADAM
         GEORGE aged 27.

----

156   Erected by ALEXANDER SKENE Crossfold in memory of his wife ISABELLA GEORGE
         d.19 June 1920 aged 70, above ALEXANDER SKENE d.19 Jan.1933 aged 83.

----

157   (Heart) SKENE. In loving memory of dear little ALICE d.21 Jan.1919 aged 4½.

----

158   Sacred to the memory of LEWIS younger son of WILLIAM SKENE contractor d.20 Jan.1872
         aged 19. His dau. MAGGIE ANN d.17 Sept.1874 aged 23. MARIA C.GRANT d.10 Aug.
         1886 aged 76, above WILLIAM SKENE contractor d.28 Apr.1887 aged 65.

----

159   In loving memory of WILLIAM REID farmer Craskins d.15 Jan.1919 aged 59, his wife
         JESSIE JOAN FARQUHARSON d.23 Dec.1920 aged 51. Their son DUNCAN REID d.3
         Feb.1973 aged 78, husband of IDA MARY MITCHELL d.4 Aug.1986 aged 93. Bottom: And
         their granddau. YVONNE A.REID (BABY) d.26 May 1943 aged 14.

----

160   In memory of FORBES C.WEBSTER d.27 Oct.1917 aged 10mths. In memory of WILLIAM
         C.WEBSTER d.17 Nov.1943 at Lovat House, Tarland, his wife ELIZA ANDERSON d.16
         Sept.1950. Their dau. HELEN MARY d.25 Sept.1995, her husband ROBERT J.MILLIGAN
         d.2 Dec.1962.

----

161   In memory of my husband NORMAN M.FORBES d.22 Mar.1963 aged 55.

161a   In loving memory of our dear children GEORGE aged 3mths., CHARLIE aged 7. A mother's
         love lies there. THOMSON.

----

162   In loving memory of JOHN BIRNIE 1863 - 1932, dear husband of REBECCA CLARK 1868
         - 1950. (Shield in front) In memory of our children J.B.

----

163   In loving memory of ALEXANDER CAMERON d.25 Mar.1863 aged 38, his wife JANE
         CLARK d.Bandley, Alford 21 Sept.1912 aged 77.

----

164   (Heart) In memory of JAMES COUTTS STIRLING b.5 Nov.1882 - d.1 July 1911.

----

165   In loving memory of our mother Mrs. COUTTS d.Mulloch 25 Jan.1894 aged 77, our brother
         PETER COUTTS d.23 Nov.1887 aged 35. Our father CHARLES COUTTS d.Mulloch 18
         Feb.1913 aged 95, his grandson GEORGE COUTTS d.there 7 Dec.1922 aged 36. JANE
         ANDERSON wife of CHARLES COUTTS farmer Mulloch, Dinnet d.15 Aug.1930 aged 74,
         said CHARLES COUTTS Mulloch d.28 Feb.1931 aged 76.

----

166   In memory of WILLIAM COUTTS crofter Mulloch d.8 Oct.1895 aged 77, JANET
         ANDERSON his wife d.26 Dec.1891 aged 63. Of their children ISABELLA d.19 Jan.1874
         aged 16, ROBERT d.19 July 1871 aged 21, ALEXANDER husband of ANNIE SMITH
         d.Cambus O'May 27 Nov.1904 aged 41.

----

167   In loving memory of our dear father ROBERT COUTTS farmer Kirkhill, Migvie d.24 Jan.
         1906 aged 78, his wife HELEN ANDERSON d.23 Sept.1929 at Ley, Towie aged 82. In
         loving remembrance also of their son ROBERT COUTTS d.23 May 1960 aged 83, his wife
         JEANNIE STEPHEN d.30 Apr.1951 aged 64.

168 In memory of JANE THOMSON Tarland d.27 Feb.1908 aged 70, her sister MARGARET THOMSON d.21 July 1909 aged 68. THOMAS THOMSON weaver Tarland, father of above d.7 May 1876 & his wife MARGARET COUTTS d.11 Mar.1876. Their son JOHN d.25 July 1861 aged 21.

---

169 In loving memory of our father & mother WILLIAM BREMNER contractor Drimmie, his wife JANE ANDERSON also their dau. MARGARET d.20 Jan.1937. Their son WILLIAM husband of MARGARET CLARK d.Coynach, Migvie 21 Mar.1941 aged 82. Above MARGARET CLARK d.there 21 Mar.1955 aged 89. Their dau. ANNIE d.23 Apr.1971, their son WILLIAM d.19 Mar.1979. Bottom: MARGARET ANDERSON sister of above JANE ANDERSON.

---

170 Erected by GEORGE McWILLIAM in loving memory of his mother ANNIE THOW d.Boghead, Tarland 5 Aug.1909 aged 79. Her mother HELEN DAVIDSON wife of JOHN THOW farmer Tillygarmonth, Birse. (No details - there seems to be a line missing) & is interred here. Above GEORGE McWILLIAM gardener d.Kirkland House, Banchory 12 July 1934 aged 73. His uncle GEORGE STRACHAN Drummy, Tarland d.22 June 1888 aged 82.

---

171 Erected in memory of JAMES ROBERTSON Mill of Newton, Coldstone d.20 July 1843 aged 60, his wife ISABEL ROBERTSON d.Ballater 21 Apr.1816. His 2nd wife ISABEL REID d.Mill of Newton 4 Mar.1869 aged 79. Their son JOHN d.1 Jan.1893 aged 70, their dau. JANE d.17 Sept.1895 aged 75.

---

172 In loving memory of JESSIE COUTTS wife of DUNCAN CUMMING d.Park House, Tarland 7 Jan.1902 aged 62. His son WILLIAM d.Bulawayo, S.A. 13 July 1912 aged 40. Above DUNCAN CUMMING d.Forbes Cottage, Tarland 18 July 1917 aged 78. His dau. MARY wife of PETER LOW d.there 20 July 1944 aged 81. Base: Erected by her husband & family.

---

173 (Marker type) 1821 W.R. I.F.

---

174 In loving memory of ISABELLA MACKIE Wellgrove, Aboyne d.6 Sept.1959 aged 82, dear mother of ROSIE. Above ROSALINE AMELIA ROBERTSON d.17 Oct.1986 aged 77.

---

175 Erected by JOHN & CATHERINE KELLAS West Chrad, Coull in memory of their dear children ELSIE JEANNIE d.8 Dec.1902 aged 3, CHARLES d.21 Aug.1906 aged 8. Above CATHERINE wife of JOHN KELLAS d.Greystone, Logie Coldstone 29 Nov.1929 aged 56. Above JOHN KELLAS d.18 June 1962 aged 91.

---

176 In memory of CHARLES CLARK Tillygarmond, Finzean d.4 Nov.1932 aged 77, his wife HELEN TAYLOR d.16 May 1953 aged 89. Their son ALEXANDER d.Woodend Hospital 9 Jan.1968.

---

177 In memory of GEORGE CLARK Mill of Corrachree d.24 Jan.1889 aged 77, his wife JANE McCOMBIE d.13 June 1873 aged 54. Their sons DONALD d.Thorold, Ontario, Canada 22 Feb.1886 aged 37, DAVID d.Kimberly, S.Africa 23 Oct.1887 aged 34, ANDREW d.in Australia aged 32, JAMES d.their (sic) also aged 51, WILLIAM d.Tillygarmond, Finzean 2 Apr.1931 aged 81 & is interred here. Base: Erected by the surviving members of the family.

---

178 Erected by ALEXANDER COPLAND in memory of his mother ISOBELLA FYFE d.Kirktown Aboyne 2 June 1870 aged 42. His grandmother ISOBELLA MORRICE d.23 Apr.1885 aged 95.

----

179 Erected by JAMES & LENA McCONNACH in loving memory of their daus. ISABELLA WALKER d.4 Nov.1915 aged 1yr 7mths., BLANCHE BENSON d.12 May 1933 aged 16 days. Above JAMES McCONNACH d.24 June 1954 aged 68, above LENA McCONNACH d.3 Apr.1980 aged 87.

----

180 In memory of JOHN KESSON sometime farmer in Dauch, Coldstone & latterly in Upper-Drummalachie in Towie d.19 Dec.1843 aged 85. His 1st wife JANET STRACHAN d.in 1801 aged 45, his 2nd wife JANE KESSON d.Upper Drummalachie, Towie 2 Feb.1864 aged 92. Her neice (sic) JANE KESSON d.Drummie, Tarland 2 Apr.1895 aged 84. Erected by their surviving family.

----

181 In loving memory of JOHN KESSON late farmer at Broombrae, Corrachree d.20 Jan.1862 aged 72, his wife ANN SIMPSON d.The Commercial Inn, Tarland 24 Feb.1879 aged 82. Their 2 sons WILLIAM d.Broombrae, Corrachree 12 Oct.1858 aged 24, JOHN d.Mains of Hopewell 25 June 1867 aged 34.

----

182 In loving memory of CHARLES INGRAM COPLAND retired farmer late of Oldtown, Tarland d.7 Jan.1969 at Ailsa, Tarland. ANNIE HENDERSON COPLAND d.4 June 1970 there. Also her son HARRY McROBB COPLAND d.6 Mar.1995 there.

----

183 In memory of ANDREW MILNE Drummy, Tarland d.27 Oct.1899 aged 77.

----

184 In memory of ALEXANDER ILLINGWORTH late of Newmill, Tarland d.2 Oct.1926 aged 86. His dau. KATE McLEAN wife of J.T.GIROUX d.Vancouver 10 Mar.1929 aged 46. ANNIE CUMMING wife of FREDERICK SPENCE d.Aberdeen 6 Nov.1933 aged 44. MARY CUMMING wife of above d.13 July 1936 aged 79.

(Heart by church wall) Our dear brother ALICK.

----

185 (Flat) Erected in memory of JAMES MANN late dyer in Tarland dep.10 Mar.1833 in 70th year and his spouse MARGRET RANNIE d.12 Sept.1838 aged 76.

----

186 (Flat - This is very worn - deciphered with the help of Jervise & Scott's Fasti) In memory of GEORGE WATSON (son of) the Rev. ANDREW WATSON minister of the Gospel Tarland. A youth of great promise..../....Christian and..... scholar d.(22) Nov.1819 in the (18th year of his age & 4th of his) Academic s....(at Marischall College.) Also of MARGARET OGILVIE WATSON his youngest sister d.(29) Aug.1827 aged 13. Also of HELEN WATSON their beloved & affectionate mother d.10 Mar.1837 aged 67 and of ANDREW WATSON (FORDYCE of Ardoe, advocate in Aberdeen) their youngest son d.4 Apr.1837 (in the 26th) year of his age. 2 lines Latin.

----

187 In memory of my uncle WILLIAM TAYLOR d.27 Jan.1922.

----

188 In memory of the Rev. ANDREW WATSON minister of the Gospel at Tarland d.9 Mar.1845 in 82nd year of his age & 46th of his ministry. HELEN MAITLAND his wife d.10 Mar.1837 in 67th year. ELIZABETH his eldest dau. d.7 Mar.1848 aged 43.

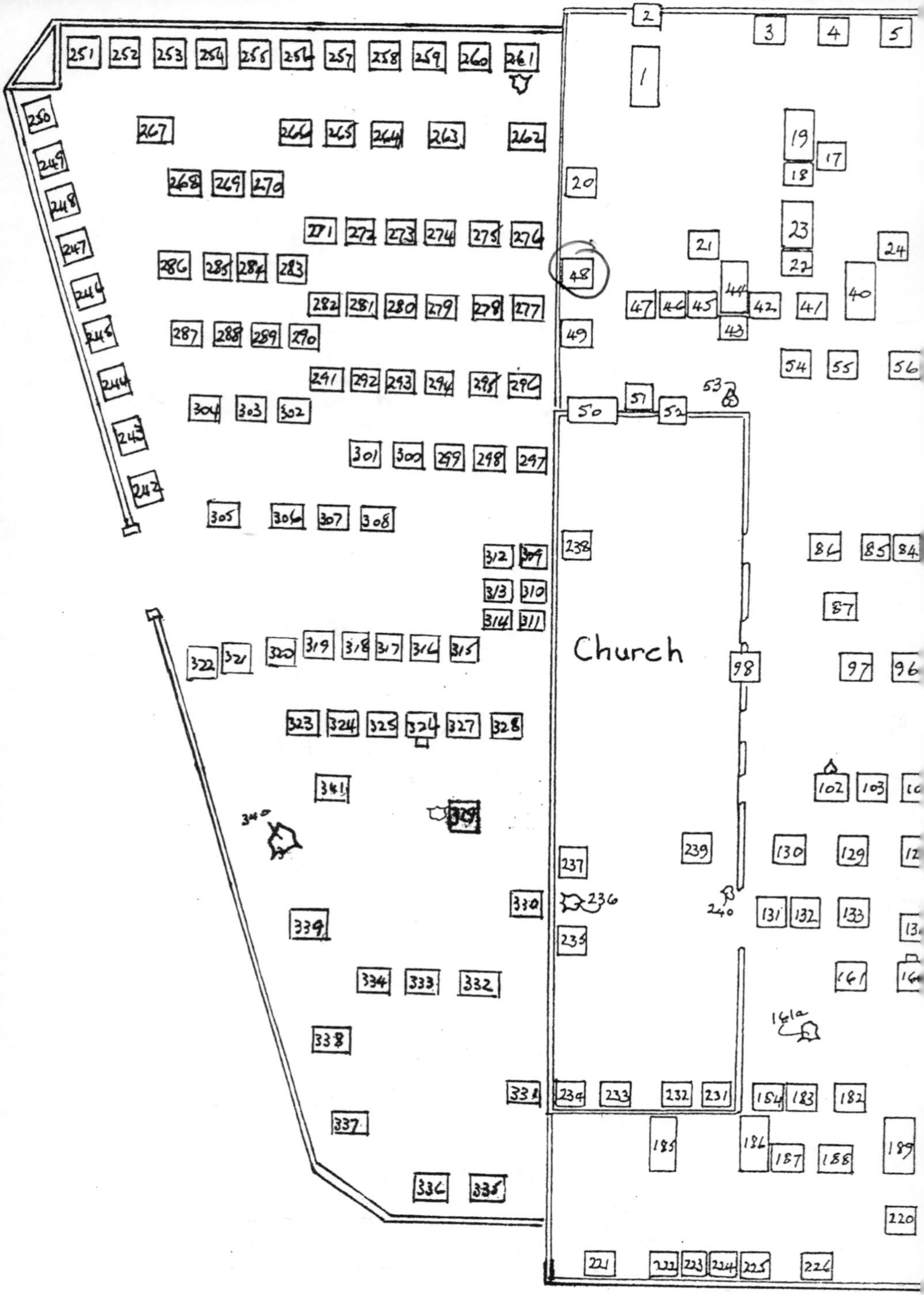

Church
1
2
3
4
5
17
18
19
20
21
22
23
24
40
41
42
43
44
45
46
47
48
49
50
51
52
53
54
55
56
84
85
86
87
96
97
98
102
103
129
130
131
132
133
161
161a
182
183
184
185
186
187
188
189
220
221
222
223
224
225
226
231
232
233
234
235
236
237
238
239
240
242
243
244
245
246
247
248
249
250
251
252
253
254
255
256
257
258
259
260
261
262
263
264
265
266
267
268
269
270
271
272
273
274
275
276
277
278
279
280
281
282
283
284
285
286
287
288
289
290
291
292
293
294
295
296
297
298
299
300
301
302
303
304
305
306
307
308
309
310
311
312
313
314
315
316
317
318
319
320
321
322
323
324
325
326
327
328
329
330
331
332
333
334
335
336
337
338
339
340
341

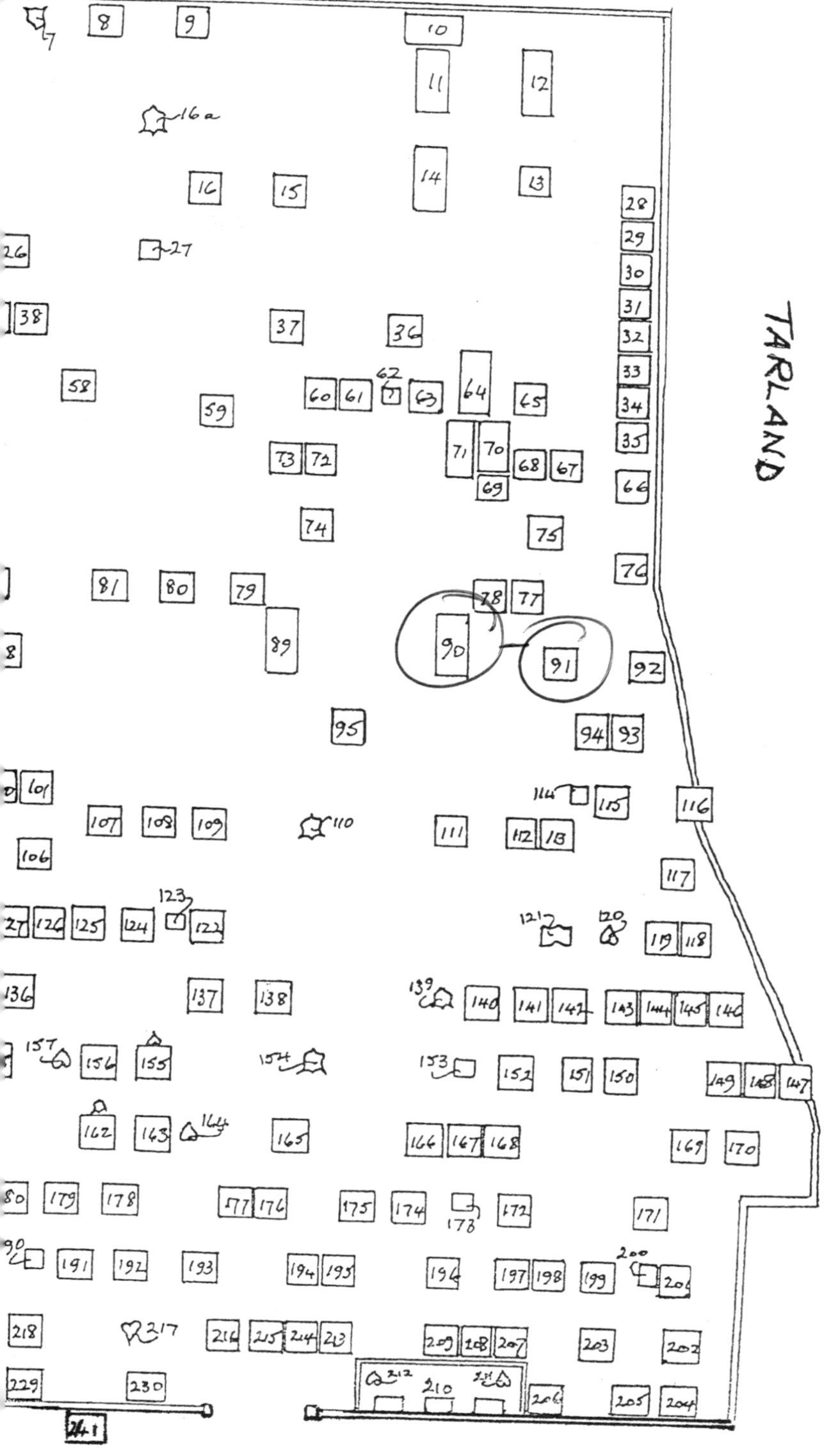
TARLAND
7
8
9
10
11
12
16a
14
13
16
15
28
29
30
31
32
33
34
35
26
27
38
37
36
62
58
60
61
63
64
65
59
73
72
71
70
68
67
69
66
74
75
76
81
80
79
78
77
89
90
91
92
8
95
94
93
101
114
115
116
107
108
109
110
111
112
113
106
117
123
27
126
125
124
122
121
120
119
118
136
137
138
139
140
141
142
143
144
145
146
157
156
155
154
153
152
151
150
149
148
147
162
163
164
165
166
167
168
169
170
80
179
178
177
176
175
174
173
172
171
190
191
192
193
194
195
196
197
198
199
200
201
218
217
216
215
214
213
209
208
207
203
202
229
230
212
210
211
206
205
204
241

189 (Flat) In memory of WILLIAM WATSON farmer in Easter Knowhead, son of the Rev. ANDREW WATSON d.15 Jan.1852 aged 45. Also ELISABETH ROSS or WATSON his widow d.there 28 Aug.1880 in her 80th year.

---

190 (Small square inset) FYFE. In memory of my loved ones d.1 July 1922 & 25 Feb. 1936.

---

191 In loving memory of my dear husband & Dad ROBERT GAULD d.8 Sept.1980 aged 70 also a dear wife & Mum SARAH PETRIE d.10 May 1993 aged 83.

---

192 Erected by GEORGE CALDER in memory of his wife JESSIE ANN DAVIDSON d.22 Nov. 1922 aged 44. Their daus. JESSIE d.4 Jan.1926 aged 21, ANN d.7 Feb.1933 aged 30. Above GEORGE CALDER d.30 Mar.1952 aged 75. Also their dau. MARTHA d.29 Apr.2000 aged 84.

---

193 To the memory of ALEXANDER DUNCAN square-wright Tarland d.22 Jan.1842 aged 29. His mother JANE McCONDACH d.10 June 1842 aged 58. WILLIAM WATSON druggist d. 16 Jan.1873 aged 72, his wife ANN DUNCAN d.10 Aug.1867 aged 53.

---

194 In loving memory of HARRY WILLIAMS farmer Mains of Kincraigie d.15 Dec.1922 aged 72. JANE RIACH wife of above d.17 Feb.1936 aged 80. Their eldest son GEORGE d.11 Jan.1970 aged 85.

---

195 In loving memory of GEORGE FYFE tailor d.3 Oct.1934 aged 58, his wife MARIA FYFE d.6 Dec.1956 aged 72. Their dau. MARY d.12 Dec.1934 aged 20, their son JOHN d.16 Dec. 1922 aged 3. Bottom: Erected by the family.

---

196 Erected by JAMES GRANT shoemaker in memory of his wife ANN HENDERSON d.6 May 1925 aged 75. His son ROBERT was killed in France 31 July 1917 aged 25. Above JAMES GRANT d.18 Jan.1933 aged 78. His dau. ISABELLA MILNE d.27 Mar.1954 aged 67.

---

197 In affectionate remembrance of GEORGE GORDON Tarland d.12 Sept.1886 aged 56. ROBERT his son d.8 Mar.1866 aged 6, ANNIE his dau. d.in infancy 5 Jan.1877. His sons SKENE GORDON M.D., d.Grahamstown, South Africa 2 Aug.1884 aged 27, GEORGE farmer in Mill of Newton d.14 Nov.1901 aged 36. MARY ILLINGWORTH widow of said GEORGE GORDON d.Tarland 15 Dec.1919 aged 84.

---

198 Erected by GEORGE GORDON blacksmith Tarland in memory of his wife CHRISTIAN MESSON d.8 June 1861 aged 62. Their son ROBERT d.7 Jan.1861 aged 20. Above GEORGE GORDON d.Tarland 19 June 1866 aged 66.

---

199 1879. JANE WILSON.

---

200 In loving memory of CHRISSY d.in infancy, NELLIE aged 1, WILLIAM aged 20.

---

201 In loving memory of MARGARET SIM wife of ALEXANDER MORREN merchant Tarland d.17 Sept.1912 aged 53. Above ALEXANDER MORREN d.23 June 1935 aged 83.

---

202 In loving memory of JAMES G.MORRICE d.22 Nov.1931 aged 72. His children CHRISTINA & HELEN d.in infancy, WILLIAM aged 20, JOHN aged 9, ALEXANDER aged 16. His wife ANNE THOMSON d.24 Mar.1959 aged 91. Their son HUGH d.26 Aug.1962/

202cont./aged 58. Their dau. CHRISTINA DONALDSON d.18 Aug.1996 aged 86.

---

203 In loving memory of our father WILLIAM CROMAR d.Boghead, Aboyne 4 June 1918 aged 56, our mother JEAN CRAWFORD d.Mill of Dinnet, Dinnet 8 Apr.1940 aged 74. Their eldest son WILLIAM CROMAR d.5 July 1961 aged 73, their 3rd son ALEXANDER CROMAR d.22 Jan.1973 aged 80.

---

204 In loving memory of LIZZIE wife of ANDREW SKENE merchant Tarland d.10 Mar.1887 aged 36. Their son HENRY d.26 Aug.1877 aged 6mths. & JAMES d.22 Nov.1889 aged 2yrs 9mths. THOMAS d.5 Mar.1890 aged 7. Above ANDREW SKENE d.Tarland 6 June 1901 aged 54. WILLIAM HENRY son of above d.Bethlehem, South Africa 12 Feb 1908 aged 32. (Heart) Our dear Mamma.

---

205 In loving memory of ARTHUR SKENE Sergt. 4th Gordons killed at Arras 1917 aged 22. Base: PAT SKENE Pte. 6th Seaforths killed at Courtrai 1918 aged 28?

---

206 In memory of JOHN W.THOMSON d.9 July 1871 aged 73, his son JOHN ALEXANDER d. in infancy. JANE TAWSE wife of above d.3 Nov.1878 aged 73. Their daus. ANN d.12 Dec. 1879 aged 50, CATHERINE d.Melbourne 16 Mar.1890 aged 49, MARGARET d.9 Aug.1897 aged 53. Their son WILLIAM d.Warrnambool, Australia 10 Oct.1914 aged 83. JAMES THOMSON J.P., Fawsyde d.8 Oct.1917 aged 80.

---

207 In affectionate remembrance of JOHN SKEEN innkeeper Tarland d.10 Apr.1882 aged 57. ANN KESSON his wife d.6 Sept.1927 aged 89.

---

208 In memory of JOHN SKEEN merchant Tarland d.28 Dec.1870 aged 76, his wife ANN MOIR d.27 Dec.1870 aged 71. At Ringwood Cottage, Cults JAMES SKEEN d.6 Nov.1882 aged 42. At Kasauli, India ANDREW SKEEN Surgeon Major MB.,IMD d.10 June 1885 aged 43. At Aberdeen WILLIAM SKEEN Deputy Surgeon General MD.,LRCS.d.2 Apr.1886 aged 53. (RHS) ANN dau. of JOHN SKEEN & wife of JOHN STEVENSON merchant Aberdeen d.12 Sept.1857 aged 29. At Sarnia, Canada JANE SKEEN wife of GEORGE LEYS d.7 Sept.1881 aged 53. At Turriff HELEN SKEEN wife of JOHN DAVIE d.17 May 1885 aged 50. At Sea Park, Port Shepsone, Natal MARGARET SKEEN wife of PATRICK DICKSON d.25 Mar. 1890 aged 59. (LHS) At Burnside, Drumlithie GEORGE SKEEN d.21 May 1907 aged 70. At Balmoral Place, Aberdeen ISABELLA SKEEN d.28 Jan.1914 aged 90.

---

209 Erected by ISABELLA SKEEN in memory of ANN SKEEN wife of JOHN STEPHENSON also of GEORGE JOHN & WILLIAM infant sons of GEORGE SKEEN. 1900.

---

210 (Triptych) (LHS) In memory of DUNCAN ROBERTSON formerly of Blairgowrie d.Indego, the residence of his son 27 Feb.1851 aged 77. Also of DUNCAN ROBERTSON of Hopewell, late of the Foreign Office, son of ANDREW ROBERTSON M.D., b.7 Aug.1838 - d.6 Apr. 1907. 2 lines text. (Centre) In memory of ANDREW ROBERTSON M.D.of Hopewell, for many years Commissioner on Deeside for Her Majesty the Queen, H.R.H. the Prince Consort & H.R.H. the Prince of Wales b.8 Apr.1799 - d.16 Nov.1881. His wife ANN FARQUHARSON dau. of JAMES FARQUHARSON in Belnabodach b.1808 - d.31 Aug. 1842 - interred Crathie Churchyard. Bottom: 3 lines text. (LHS)In memory of ANNE SWETE 2nd wife of ANDREW ROBERTSON of Hopewell, dau. of Rev. JOHN SWETE in Oxton, Devon b.28 Feb.1800 - d.30 May 1868 also ANDREW ROBERTSON WILSON M.D., sometime of Hopewell d.25 June 1932.

211 (Shield) ANNIE LOUISA WILSON R.R.C., d.26 Apr.1937 aged 71.

---

212 (Shield) ALICE WILSON wife of ANDREW R.WILSON M.D., d.16 Sept.1951 aged 81.

---

213 In memory of ANN EWEN wife of PETER SUMMERS d.West Town 31 Dec.1875 aged 50. Their 3rd son JAMES d.2 Apr.1889 aged 22. PETER SUMMERS d.Woodend, Melgum 24 Dec.1919 aged 84, his widow MARGARET MICHIE d.15 July 1923 aged 85.

---

214 In memory of JOHN EWEN d.30 Jan.1917 aged 74, his wife ISIE FERRIES d.20 Feb.1939 aged 80. Their family ROBINA d.26 Dec.1900 aged 16, GEORGE fell in action 15 June 1918 aged 22, LOVINA d.30 Sept.1931 aged 29, WILLIAM d.in infancy.

---

215 In loving memory of ROBERT EWEN farmer Westtown, Tarland d.27 Jan.1890 aged 70 his wife ANN EWEN d.2 July 1890 aged 78. Their son JAMES d.23 Aug.1868 aged 16yrs 11mths. Base: Erected by their family.

---

216 Erected by ISABELLA THOMSON in memory of her husband JAMES EWEN farmer Millhead d.31 Dec.1890 aged 61. Above ISABELLA THOMSON d.28 Jan.1897 aged 63.

---

217 (Heart) WILLIAMS.

---

218 In loving memory of WILLIAM SHARP d.3 Aug.1913, his wife MARTHA BRUCE d.24 Aug. 1914. Their sons JAMES d.27 Nov.1951, WILLIAM d.24 Dec.1954. Their daus. JEANNIE d.22 Nov.1946, AGNES d.4 Sept.1964.

---

219 Erected 1879 in memory of HARRY THOMSON carpenter Old Mill, Tarland d.15 Aug. 1858 aged 56. His wife JANE WILLIAMS d.8 Mar.1862 aged 46. Their grandchild JAMES R.THOMSON d.Aberdeen 11 Jan.1881 aged 2yrs 6mths. Their son-in-law JAMES RUGG d.Inverurie 20 Mar.1889 aged 42. Bottom: 2 lines text. Base: Erected by their family.

---

220 1863. Erected by ROBERT THOMSON farmer in Old Mill, Tarland in memory of his wife JANNET WILLIAM d.28 Apr.1863 aged 59. His dau. ELISABETH d.10 May 1850 aged 20. His son CHARLES d.20 Dec.1861 aged 20. Above ROBERT THOMSON d.12 June 1877 aged 86.

---

221 In memory of our father JOHN CUMMING d.Rhin Mhor, Tarland 26 Jan.1921 aged 77, his son ALICK d.7 Feb.1894 aged 21 & other members of his family. His dau. MARY d.27 May 1951. His wife ANN WATT d.24 May 1962 - both d.in Edinburgh. His dau. ANNIE d.there 31 Dec.1971.

---

222 In memory of JOHN TAWSE gardener Corachree (sic) d.6 Feb.1908 aged 59, his wife MARGARET KERR d.Mill of Newton 30 June 1939 aged 89.

---

223 In loving memory of ALEXANDER HEPBURN blacksmith Tarland d.4 May 1920 aged 71. His daus. ISABELLA d.27 June 1889 aged 13mths., ANNIE d.Aberdeen 12 Sept.1925 (no age given) BARBARA REID his wife d.21 Apr.1928 aged 76. His dau. BARBARA d.Bridge Cottage 23 Jan.1943, his youngest dau. ROBINA d.Aberdeen 12 Dec.1950.

---

223 Erected by the family in loving memory of ISABELLA ANN PROFEIT wife of JOHN COUTTS Woodend, Melgum d.14 July 1907 aged 77. The above JOHN COUTTS d.there 5/

223cont./June 1914 aged 87. Bottom: 1 line text.

224 Erected by JAMES COUTTS in loving memory of his wife JANE FORBES d.Milton Braes, Logie Coldstone 3 Oct.1929 aged 57. Their son ROBERT R.A.F.aged 28 d.30 May 1941. Above JAMES COUTTS d.Forbes Cottage, Tarland 12 Jan.1949 aged 81. Their son ALEXANDER FORBES COUTTS d.5 Jan.1972 aged 69, their eldest dau. ROSE ANN d.4 Dec.1978 aged 81, their dau. CATHERINE d.5 Nov.1990 aged 90.

226 In loving memory of MARGARET DONALDSON wife of ROBERT THOMSON Broomhill, Tarland d.12 June 1901 aged 71. Above ROBERT THOMSON d.4 Feb.1921 aged 87. CHARLES BAIN late of Boig, Tarland d.Nithsdale, Kemnay 23 May 1927 aged 75. ISABELLA LEYS his widow d.Foggieley, Corse 24 Oct.1933 aged 82.

227 In loving memory of our father ISAAC GILCHRIST FRASER d.Muirton, Corse 11 Mar.1906 aged 71, our mother ELIZABETH MILNE d.Firhurst, Aboyne 17 Oct.1917 aged 70.

228 In loving memory of ANN FRASER wife of GEORGE MASSON d.Schoolhill, Tarland 12 Oct.1896 aged 59. Said GEORGE MASSON d.Newton of Mulloch, Dinnet 7 Apr.1928 aged 85. Their son ISAAC GILCHRIST MASSON d.Tarland 29 Nov.1925 aged 62, his wife ELIZABETH WILSON d.26 Nov.1957 aged 94.

229 1899. In memory of JOHN EMSLIE carpenter Tarland d.18 Nov.1898 aged 58. His wife MARY ANN McKENZIE d.Glasgow 19 Apr.1880 aged 38. HELEN JANE EMSLIE d.27 Apr.1902 aged 11mths., also JOHN & JEANNIE, twins d.in infancy - children of JAMES EMSLIE. JANET BIRSS d.31 Mar.1931 aged 83 also wife of above JOHN EMSLIE. HELEN SIM wife of JAMES EMSLIE d.1 Nov.1935 aged 69.

230 Erected by JAMES JOHNSTON in loving memory of his dau. JEANNIE JOHNSTON d.Hillhead, Tarland 1 Oct.1889 aged 19. Said JAMES JOHNSTON d.Banchory 4 Feb.1907 aged 55, his youngest son HENERY (sic) HALDANE DONAL d.18 Oct.1918 aged 32. ANN SMITH wife of first named d.Banchory 21 Oct.1940 aged 85.

231 (Heart) In memory of ALEXANDER McKIDDIE aged 32.

232 In memory of JAMES WILLIAM SKENE husband of JANE FORBES d.20 Jan.1942 aged 75 above JANE FORBES d.11 May 1944 aged 76.

233 Erected by JAMES SKENE Knowhead in loving memory of his son ROBERT d.14 Aug. 1881 aged 22. His wife ANN TAYLOR d.7 Mar.1891 aged 62. Above JAMES SKENE d. Tarland 5 June 1891 aged 62. (Heart) In memory of ROBERT SKENE.

234 In memory of ROBERT URE farmer Melgum, Tarland b.8 Dec.1827 - d.27 Feb.1892.

235 Erected by Mrs. ROSS & family in affectionate remembrance of JAMES ROSS d. Douneside, Tarland 7 Oct.1887 aged 60. His son WILLIAM d.Cape Nome, Alaska 1 Jan. 1901 aged 32. His wife MARY ANN GALL d.Viewington, Ballater 12 Sept.1903 aged 67. Their son GEORGE MURRAY d.Aberdeen 9 Jan.1926 aged 56, their dau. MARY ANNE d.Viewington, Ballater 20 Jan.1928 aged 54. Their eldest son JAMES d.Aberdeen 13 June 1933 aged 67. Plinth: And AMELIA GALL BARRON last surviving member d.Aberdeen 2 May 1939 aged 67. Base: 2 lines verse.

236 In loving memory of CHARLES SKENE late farmer Culsh d.Ballater 2 Mar.1920 aged 82, his wife ANN PIRIE d.Glenmuick 6 Dec.1927 aged 82. Their family: MARGARET & JAMES d.at Culsh (no details), CHARLES d.Kalinova, the Balkans 15 Sept.1918 aged 32. ANN SKENE d.Linn of Muick, Glenmuick, Ballater 12 Nov.1934 aged 61. Bottom: Erected by the family.

----

237 (Shield) GRASSICK.

----

238 In loving memory of our father JOHN GRASSICK d.28 Dec.1886 aged 42, our mother JANE FLORENCE d.24 Apr.1900 aged 51. Our brother WILLIAM d.23 July 1934 aged 59.

----

239 Erected by ROBERT R.H.AUSTIN in memory of his son ROBERTIE (sic) d.16 Aug.1879 aged 23mths. Back. 1 line text. And of ANNIE GORDON his wife d.5 June 1883 aged 30. 4 lines verse.

----

240 In memory of ANDREW ROSS J.P. 3rd son of HARRY ROSS some time farmer in Wester Coull who discharged the duties of factor for 40 years on the estates of the EARL of ABOYNE in Cromar with such judgement, integrity & kindness that he enjoyed the full confidence of the proprietor and the universal respect of the tenants. He d.17 May 1870 aged 76. (LHS) ALEXANDER ROSS his brother and farmer in Oldtown of Kincraigie d.12 Feb. 1885 aged 82.

----

241 (This stone is outside the churchyard, on top of the bank. It is beautifully carved depicting a violin and a sheet of music.) Dedicated to the memory of PETER MILNE. A famous violinist and composer of Scottish music. 1824 - 1908. Erected by a grateful public. Base: 2 lines verse.

Into the newer section at the far side of the Church.

242 In loving memory of CHARLES H.CROMAR farmer Glack, Tarland d.1 Oct.1975 beloved husband of ELIZABETH FORBES.

----

243 In loving memory of my dear husband LENNOX HOWELL d.9 Mar.1946.

----

244 In loving memory of JOHN ESSON b.Braehead, Tarland, a veteran of the Wet Review, d.Edinburgh 13 June 1952 aged 91.

----

245 In loving memory of my dear husband & our father JOHN McCOMBIE d.Davan 27 Apr. 1948 aged 74, his wife MARY STRACHAN RIACH d.19 June 1950 aged 75. Their son CHARLES FORBES d.4 May 1963 aged 62.

----

246 In loving memory of a dear husband & father WILLIAM BEGG Cauldhame, Cushnie, Alford d.10 Aug.1948 aged 69. His dau. HELEN ANNE d.Foresterhill 16 Feb.1957 aged 46. His beloved wife MARY McBAIN d.Elrick Cottage, Stonehaven 26 Sept.1957 aged 74.

----

247 In loving memory of JOHN McCOMBIE beloved husband of ELIZABETH BRUCE d.Abergairn, Ballater 24 Feb.1949 aged 77. His beloved wife ELIZABETH BRUCE d.Invergelder Cottages, Crathie 2 June 1963 aged 75. Ever remembered.

----

248 Erected to the memory of WILLIAM SMITH beloved husband of MARY SMITH, d.as result of an accident at Lonach Hall, Strathdon 20 Oct.1949 aged 61. Above MARY SMITH d.5 Burnett Place, Aberdeen 21 Oct.1966 aged 71. 1 line text.

----

249 To the dear memory of ALEXANDER SMITH farmer Home Farm, Corrachree d.5 June 1953 aged 84 beloved husband of MARY LINDSAY who d.13 Oct.1960 aged 86. Their dau. ELIZABETH ROSS (BESSIE) d.15 Dec.1964 aged 66. JANE ARCHIBALD (JEAN) d.2 May 1990 aged 77.

----

250 In loving memory of JESSIE SMITH wife of the late JAMES P.GARIOCH d.12 Sept.1987 aged 77.

----

251 In memory of JOHN JOHNSTON Broomfield, Drummie, Tarland d.22 Jan.1955 aged 81.

----

252 In loving memory of ISABELLA ANN RITCHIE beloved wife of ALEXANDER SHARP d.10 Aug.1938 aged 50. Above ALEXANDER SHARP d.13 Sept.1970 aged 81.

----

253 Erected by JOHN GRANT shoemaker in memory of his wife ELSPETH SANDISON d.26 Oct. 1943 & their son SANDY d.7 Aug.1938. Also his 2nd wife HANNAH JOHNSON d.22 Nov. 1964. Above JOHN GRANT d.5 Mar.1970.

----

254 In loving memory of my dear husband KEITH G.CRYLE d.31 May 1988 aged 75.

----

255 In memory of MARGARET ANN MARTIN d.Tarland 22 Aug.1937 beloved wife of WILLIAM GRASSICK. Above WILLIAM GRASSICK d.24 May 1940.

----

256 In loving memory of GEORGE MORGAN THOM d.28 Feb.1965 aged 81 beloved husband of EDITH DUGUID d.17 Oct.1988 aged 96. Bottom: Erected by wife & family.

----

257 In loving memory of JOHN STEWART blacksmith beloved husband of HELEN BURNETT d.Marywell, Lumphanan 10 Nov.1936 in 33rd year. Also our beloved dau. HELEN BARBARA b.9 May 1930 - d.11 Apr.1933. Above HELEN BURNETT d.11 July 1973 aged 68, widow of ALFRED MICHIE M.N. lost at sea 1942.

----

258 In loving memory of GEORGE McALLAN beloved husband of CATHERINE MASSIE d.3 Aug. 1960 aged 71. Also the above, our beloved Mam d.24 Nov.1993 aged 97.Also their youngest son JAMES ALEXANDER (SANDY) d.27 Oct.2001 aged 73. Bottom: Erected by his widow & family.

----

259 In loving memory of JOHN CALDER Parkview, Tarland d.19 Dec.1967 aged 66 beloved husband of BARBARA ANN ROSS d.19 Jan.1986 aged 85. Also their dau. PHYLLIS d.28 Nov. 1932 aged 5 & their son JOHN d.in infancy.

----

260 (Shield) LOW. In memory of my loved ones. d.12 Jan.1932, 2 Jan.1946. Also 21 Feb.1950.

----

261 In memory of JOHN DUGUID 1888-1930, GEORGINA DUGUID née LAING 1887-1976. (Shield) Erected by the Tarland Junior Red Cross in memory of their loved comrade & secretary GORDON DUGUID b.1918 - d.28 July 1932. 1 line text.

262 In loving memory of our dear father DONALD GRANT d.Banchory 10 Sept.1893 aged 35 & was interred there. Also our dear mother MARY FORBES beloved wife of the above d.Tarland 5 Mar.1934 aged 75. Also our youngest sister BEATRICE d.Edinburgh 10 June 1948 aged 57.

---

263 Erected by WILLIAM GEORGE WATT in loving remembrance of his wife MARY MARGARET FYFE d.12 Dec.1934 aged 20.

---

264 In loving memory of GWLADYS (sic) PATERSON d.3 Oct.1934 aged 37 & of her husband ALEXANDER HEPBURN blacksmith d.11 Nov.1958 aged 79. Also their son Cpl. ALEXANDER HEPBURN d.abroad 9 Feb.1956 aged 36. Bottom: Erected by the family.

---

265 In loving memory of ISABELLA J.SIM beloved wife of WM. MIDDLETON d.Sweet Briar, Tarland 28 Dec.1933 aged 60. Their son JOHN killed in France 18 June 1915 aged 21. Also WILLIAM JAMES killed in France 9 Apr.1917 aged 20. Also PETER d.Adelaide 16 Oct.1936 aged 41. Above WILLIAM MIDDLETON d.Sweet Briar, Tarland 4 July 1941 aged 75. ELIZABETH INNES (Granny) d.14 Mar.1946 aged 100.

---

266 In loving memory of RICHARD GEORGE GREEN Sweet Briar, Tarland d.25 May 1981 aged 82 dearly loved husband of ISABELLA MIDDLETON d.20 Feb.2001 aged 98. Dear parents of ANN & INNES.

---

267 In loving memory of ETHEL EMSLIE d.12 Aug.1968 aged 60 beloved wife of ALBERT BIRNIE d.21 Jan.1979 aged 71.

---

268 In loving memory of a dear husband & dad ALEXANDER SMITH d.21 Dec.1985 aged 80. Also his dear wife LILLIE ANN FINDLAY d.20 Apr.1988 aged 74. (Overprinted from 84)

---

269 In loving memory of our dear son GORDON K.MORRICE d.2 Mar.1951 aged 7. Also our mother ISABELLA SUMMERS d.Woodend, Tarland 8 Apr.1960 aged 79. CHARLES A. MORRICE d.14 May 1997 aged 86, a loving father & husband of TIB. (Scroll) In loving memory of our dear son GORDON K.MORRICE d.2 Mar.1951 aged 7. (Urn) Granda.

---

270 In loving memory of ELSIE GRASSICK d.7 Hawthorn Crescent, Ballater 4 Feb.1965 aged 49 dearly beloved wife of JOHN ARCHIBALD. Also their dau. ELSIE ARCHIBALD d.7 Feb.1997 aged 58.

---

271 In loving memory of my dear husband EDWARD FORBES Tarland d.16 May 1937 aged 59. Also his beloved wife ANNIE GRANT d.4 Oct.1957 aged 80. Bottom: Erected by his widow & son.

---

272 In loving memory of my dear husband ALEXANDER McCONNACHIE d.21 Sept.1937 aged 38. Bottom: 1 line text.

---

273 Erected to the memory of ALEXANDER ANDERSON beloved husband of MARY ANN GRANT d.14 Dec.1937 aged 75 & of the above MARY ANN GRANT d.21 Nov.1939 aged 73. Also their sons ALEXANDER d.18 Oct.1895 aged 1½, JOHN d.30 Oct.1976 aged 77. Their dau. MARJORIE d.30 July 1987 aged 90.

---

274 In memory of ROBERT McCONNACHIE late of Boltenstone d.Gowanbrae 28 Dec.1937 aged 82 beloved husband of JANE ANN LORIMER. Said JANE ANN LORIMER d.there 13 Dec. 1944 aged 80.

---

275 Erected in memory of FORBES WEST JOHNSTON shoemaker Tarland d.9 Mar.1936 aged 78.

---

276 In loving memory of GEORGE ADAM shoemaker beloved husband of HELEN SMITH d.28 June 1956 aged 58. Also their infant dau. PATRICIA d.13 Apr.1934. The above HELEN W.SMITH d.7 Oct.1982 aged 76. (Urn) ADAM.

---

277 Erected in memory of ANNIE RIDDELL widow of CHARLES MESTON d.27 Nov.1938 aged 93. Also her dau. ANN MACHRAY d.Millview, Tarland 27 Apr.1959 aged 84.

---

278 In loving memory of JANE RIDDELL d.Broombrae, Corrachree, Tarland 20 Jan.1947 in 73rd yr. Also her brother ALEXANDER d.there 29 June 1942 in 78th year.

---

279 In loving memory of my dear son IAN WALKER HARPER d.St. John's Wells, Tarland 1 May 1953 aged 16. Also my dear husband HECTOR MASSON (BUNT) d.12 Aug.1979 aged 58. Bottom: 1 line text.

---

280 In loving memory of ROBERT GARIOCH d.26 Dec.1953 aged 92. His beloved wife MARGARET A.FARQUHARSON d.28 Apr.1957 aged 91.

---

281 In loving memory of WILLIAM GORDON CRAN beloved husband of MARIE COUTTS d.8 Cromar Cottages 19 Dec.1949 aged 48. Also our wee son JAMES CRAN d.28 July 1948 aged 5. His 1st wife WILLIAMINA REID d.7 Mar.1942.

---

282 In loving memory of my dear husband JOHN THOM d.25 Feb.1972 aged 68. His wife JESSIE ANN COUTTS d.21 Dec.1984 aged 81. Sadly missed.

---

283 To the dear memory of JOHN CALDER carpenter Tarland d.7 Dec.1951 aged 81 beloved husband of MARGARET THAIN. Above named MARGARET THAIN d.5 July 1958 aged 82. Their dau. HELEN d.21 Mar.1991 aged 88.

---

284 In loving memory of ROBERT ESSON farmer Strathweltie, Tarland d.21 July 1950 aged 68. His wife MARGARET STRATHDEE d.8 July 1971 aged 93. Bottom: Erected by his wife & dau.

---

285 In loving memory of MAGGIE BRUCE wife of JAMES WILLIAMS Tillyhermick, Tarland d.24 Feb.1967 aged 77. Also the above named d.30 Oct.1982 aged 83.

---

286 Erected by ALBERT E.TAYLOR in memory of his beloved wife JESSIE GRASSICK d.23 Dec. 1968 aged 56. Above ALBERT E.TAYLOR d.14 Sept.1971 aged 66. Ever remembered.

---

287 In loving memory of WILLIAM R.GIBBON d.4 Jan.1970 aged 63 beloved husband of MARY ANDERSON d.28 Jan.1986 aged 80. Also their son CYRIL d.27 Apr.1982 aged 49.

---

288 In loving memory of PENELOPE TOUGH d.25 June 1976 aged 72 beloved wife of ALEXANDER MASSON 9 Cromar Cottages, Tarland. Also the above d.8 May 1987 aged/

288cont./83. Bottom: Sadly missed.

---

289   In memory of ISABELLA EWEN d.17 Apr.1950 aged 71 beloved wife of ALEXANDER MASSON West Croft, Drummie. Above named ALEXANDER MASSON d.17 June 1953 aged 80. Bottom: Erected by husband & family.

---

290   In loving memory of our dear parents who d.Morven Villa, Tarland. JANE A.FRASER 27 Apr.1948 aged 68, ALEXANDER M.IRVINE 18 Oct.1951 aged 70.

---

291   In loving memory of my husband DAVID SMART ANDERSON Broomhill, Tarland d.9 Aug. 1968 retired factor of McRobert Estate. His wife ISABELLA S.ANDERSON d.8 Feb.1991 aged 88. Also our dear son ALLAN (ANDY) d.2 Sept.1989 aged 48. 1 line eulogy.

---

292   In loving memory of JAMES TAYLOR tailor d.The Square, Tarland 13 June 1946 aged 66. Also his son JACK Sgt. RAF lost his life over Germany 4 Dec.1944 aged 39. Also MARGARET ANN PARK beloved wife & mother d.2 Oct.1949 aged 69.

---

293   In loving memory of WILLIAM TAYLOR d.29 Mar.1970 aged 59 dear husband of ELIZABETH TAWSE.

---

294   In loving memory of ROBERT A.CROMAR d.7 Sept.1976 aged 61 beloved husband of HELEN M.ELLIS.

---

295   Treasured memories of DOUGLAS J.SMITH d.18 Nov.1990 aged 68 dear husband of BARBARA J.ROSS. (space) Also wee KENNETH d.in infancy 1952.

---

296   (Celtic Cross) In loving memory of ALEXANDER JOHN MAUNSELL MacLAUGHLIN b.Drumroe, Co.Waterford 4 Mar.1854 - d.Aboyne 9 Apr.1932. 2 lines verse.

---

297   In loving memory of our dear mother ISABELLA REID d.Calders Cottage, Tarland 24 Feb.1946 aged 66.

---

298   Sacred to the memory of JAMES R.GORDON farmer Galton, Logie Coldstone d.14 Sept.1952 beloved husband of MAGGIE JANE BREMNER d.11 Feb.1976. Their only dau. MARGARET ANN GORDON d.Romford, Essex 10 Apr.1997 aged 75, also their son-in-law ALEXANDER LESLIE Staff Sergt. REME d.Korea 18 Nov.1950 aged 28 beloved husband of MARGARET ANN GORDON.

---

299   In loving memory of PETER R.SMITH retired blacksmith Greenview, Tarland d.27 Aug.1952 aged 77 beloved husband of NICOLA LAW. Above NICOLA LAW d.16 Jan.1970 aged 88. Their youngest son PETER d.12 Apr.1975 aged 57.

---

300   In loving memory of my husband JOHN ALEXANDER KYNOCH Aberdeen Arms Hotel d.26 Sept.1950 aged 42. His beloved wife JANET McQUEEN WHYTE d.18 Oct.1983 aged 74.

---

301   To the dear memory of a beloved dau. & sister ANNIE JEAN MITCHELL (NANCY) Cromar Cottages, Tarland d.26 Mar.1949 aged 19. Also her mother ELIZABETH TAYLOR (JEAN) d.12 May 1977 aged 67.

302 In loving memory of WILLIAMINA HENDERSON d.2 July 1964 aged 82 beloved wife of ANDREW MEARNS. Above ANDREW MEARNS d.22 Dec.1965 aged 83.

----

303 In loving memory of WILLIAM ROGIE farmer Netherton, Tarland d.3 Jan.1947 aged 86. Also his wife ANN SHARP d.21 Jan.1946 aged 80. Their younger dau. LOUISA ANN d.21 Dec.1962 aged 53. Their elder dau. MARY d.6 Feb.1971 aged 71 beloved wife of Rev. THOMAS CRAWFORD d.2 May 1978 aged 73.

----

304 In memory of my dear husband WILLIAM ROGIE d.Lairg 28 Sept.1965 aged 64 & of his wife MARY COWELL GREIG d.9 Mar.2001 aged 99.

----

305 In loving memory of ALEXANDER McKENZIE d.Coreen Cottage, Tarland 29 Sept.1945 aged 76. His sons ALASTAIR d.Kenya 3 Apr.1942 aged 31, WILLIAM d.in infancy. JESSIE wife of ALEXANDER McKENZIE d.Banstead, Surrey 26 Sept.1954 aged 80. Also JOHN SIMON McKENZIE d.20 Oct.1973 aged 70, JAMES McKENZIE d.1977 aged 76. Also his dau. MARY JOHNSON d.1982 aged 88. JEAN STANTON d.1984 aged 87. Also ALAN McKENZIE d.Zambia 31 July 1985 aged 78.

----

306 (Plaque) In memory of GEORGE SLESSOR d.26 Mar.1944. His wife MAGGIE J.ROSS d.28 June 1961.

----

307 Erected by his widow & family in loving memory of JAMES MOIR farmer Upper Ruthven, Dinnet d.7 July 1949 aged 63. Also his widow RACHEL MITCHELL The Cottage, Upper Ruthven, Dinnet d.8 May 1979 aged 95. Also their 2nd son JAMES d.3 Jan.1981 aged 61.

----

308 Sacred to the memory of ALEXANDER BLACKHALL farmer Millhead, Tarland d.1 Oct.1940 aged 61 beloved husband of CATHERINE A.COUTTS. The above CATHERINE ANN COUTTS d Millhead, Tarland 23 Sept.1967 aged 93. Also their grandson SANDY d.10 Sept. 1945 aged 18mths. Their son ROBERT GEORGE d.7 Feb.1982 aged 72 beloved husband of MARY LOW. (Urn) Remembrance "wee SANDY" from Grandma & Granda. (Heart) In loving memory of our dear son wee SANDY.

----

309 (By wall) Erected by ROBERT URQUHART in memory of his beloved wife HELEN REID d.16 Feb.1954. The above ROBERT URQUHART d.25 Dec.1965 aged 86. Their dau. HELEN R. URQUHART d.2 Jan.1992 aged 78.

----

310 In loving memory of LIZZIE ANN RENNIE d.5 Oct.1965 wife of ALEXANDER McALLAN d.12 Dec.1979.

----

311 In loving memory of LYALL GRANT 23 Mar.1910 - 10 Jan.1981, CATHERINE GRANT 5 July 1911 - 8 May 1988, KENNETH GRANT 21 Apr.1945 - 20 June 1995, JEAN GRANT 2 Jan. 1906 - 5 Feb.1981, JOHN BASS GRANT 25 Aug.1900 - 10 Oct.1980, ELIZABETH WALKER 26 Jan.1908 - 21 Mar.1996.

----

312 In loving memory of MAY TROUP beloved wife of WILLIAM THOMSON d.5 Oct.1953 aged 74. Above WILLIAM THOMSON d.9 July 1956 aged 74.

----

313   In loving memory of ROBERT A.PROSSER d.19 Dec.1965 aged 53.

       In loving memory of CHARLOTTE GRIEVE d.Muirton 8 Jan.1966 aged 59 beloved wife of
314   JAMES KEMP & dear mother of VERA. Above JAMES KEMP head gamekeeper Douneside
       d.6 Dec.1987 aged 79.

----

315   Sacred to the memory of ALEXANDER TROUP d.Milton of Culsh 24 Feb.1943 aged 76 & his
       wife MARGARET WILLIAMS d.16 Mar.1957 aged 73.

----

316   Erected by EDWARD GORDON in loving memory of his wife MARY JANE McKENZIE
       d.Mill Cottage, Logie-Coldstone 23 Nov.1941 aged 39.

----

317   In loving memory of LIZZIE COOPER wife of ROBERT GRANT merchant Rothiemay d.5 June
       1941 aged 59. Said ROBERT GRANT d.27 Jan.1948 aged 77.

       Erected by ROBERT STUART in loving memory of his wife JESSIE FARQUHARSON d.12
318   Sept.1940 aged 67. Above ROBERT STUART late farmer The Parks, Logie Coldstone d.28
       Oct.1947 aged 78.

----

319   (Celtic Cross) In memory of ALEXANDER PATERSON M.A., M.B., Ch.B., b.5 Feb.1881 - d.2
       May 1933.

       In loving memory of WILLIAM ANDERSON farmer Home Farm, Hopewell, Tarland b.24 June
       1875 - d.15 May 1934 beloved husband of MAGGIE McROBERT. Their 3rd son ALEXANDER
320   McROBERT b.17 June 1907 - d.23 Nov.1910. The aforesaid MAGGIE McROBERT b.26 Sept.
       1869 - d.20 Nov.1939. Their elder dau. MAGGIE McROBERT b.8 Feb.1899 - d.9 Nov.1955.
       Their younger dau. BESSIE McROBERT b.11 July 1900 - d.5 June 1980. Base: 1 line text.

       In loving memory of my dear husband ROBERT CROMAR farmer Tillychardoch, Tarland d.15
321   Aug.1934 aged 48. His wife MARY INNES ANDERSON d.26 Feb.1946 aged 59. Bottom:
       Erected by his widow & family.

       In loving memory of ALEXANDER McCOMBIE beloved husband of ROBINA REID d.Albany,
322   Kincardine O'Neil 19 Dec.1939 aged 67. Their dau. ROBINA ALEXINA d.13 May 1946. Above
       ROBINA REID d.31 Dec.1948 aged 82. Bottom: Erected by his widow & dau.

----

323   In loving memory of GEORGE FARQUHARSON beloved husband of LILY IRVINE
       d.Lauriston, Tarland 23 June 1940 aged 31. Above LILY IRVINE d.20 Aug.1993 aged 87.

       In loving memory of WILLIAM A.CALDER carpenter Tarland beloved husband of ANNIE
324   McCONNACH d.21 Aug.1950 aged 67. Their dau. ISOBEL d.20 Jan.1936 aged 7, above
       ANNIE McCONNACH d.17 Apr.1976 aged 88.

----

325   In memory of JAMES STRACHAN d.Lochnagar, Ballater 28 Apr.1943 aged 80, his wife
       ANNIE COUTTS d.26 Jan.1961 aged 87.

       In loving memory of ALEXANDER GARIOCH d.25 July 1949 aged 86, his wife JESSIE
326   McCONNACHIE d.5 May 1943 aged 69. Their sons ALEXANDER d.27 Jan.1930 aged 27,/

326
cont. /DAVID d.13 Dec.1942 aged 28. (Plaque in front) In loving memory of JESSIE A. McCONNACHIE wife of ALEXANDER GARIOCH d.5 May 1943 aged 69.

---

327 In loving memory of EDWARD ALEXANDER son of EDWARD & ISOBEL SHERRIFFS accidentally killed 5 Jan.1944 aged 12. His father EDWARD ADAM d.1 July 1996 aged 95 beloved husband of ISOBEL MASSON Gowanlea, Lumphanan d.6 Jan.1998 aged 87.

---

328 In memory of CATHERINE SOUTER d.24 Apr.1944 aged 75 beloved wife of LEWIS McKENZIE Nether Ruthven. Their sons LEWIS GEORGE fell in action in France 16 May 1917 aged 20, ALLAN d.New Zealand 10 Feb.1942 aged 36. Above LEWIS McKENZIE farmer d.23 Dec.1955 aged 80 & their dau. ANNABEL d.12 May 1969 aged 70.

---

329 In loving memory of COLIN McGREGOR d.9 Aug.1993 aged 88 beloved husband of JESSIE GARIOCH d.13 Mar.1995 aged 85. Fondly remembered. (Shield in front) In loving memory of our beloved son JAMES COLIN MAITLAND aged 4mths. Also infant son of grandparents.

---

330 In loving memory of WILLIAM HUNTER Loanhead, Tarland for many years farmer at Oldtown d.2 Dec.1955 aged 84. His wife ALICE M.COOPER d.22 May 1962. Their younger dau. MARGARET ALICE MAY d.as the result of an accident 7 Mar.1982.

---

331 In loving memory of BATHIA ELLIS BAIRD d.2 Sept.1954 aged 47 beloved wife of WILLIAM ALEXANDER WILLIAMS. Above WILLIAM ALEXANDER WILLIAMS d.12 Oct.1978 aged 78.

---

332 In loving memory of ARTHUR C.LITTLEJOHN Sherwood, Tarland d.17 June 1978 aged 67 beloved husband of NAN COUTTS d.16 Oct.1997 aged 85. Sadly missed.

---

333 Erected by ALEXANDER FORBES in loving memory of his parents ALEXANDER FORBES d.17 June 1928, MARGARET FORGIE d.26 Aug.1924. Above ALEXANDER FORBES d.27 Mar.1967 aged 61 dear husband of ELSIE McKENZIE d.22 Dec.1989 aged 85. Their son ALEXANDER FORBES d.7 Feb.2001. (Plinth)This stone commemorates the FORBES family, butchers in Tarland for many years.

---

334 Erected by ALICE BEGG in memory of her dearly loved husband JOHN S.McKENZIE Nether Ruthven, Tarland d.25 Jan.1968 aged 55.

---

335 Erected in memory of my dear husband JAMES LAING ANDERSON Broombrae, Corrachree d.21 Sept.1954 aged 71. His beloved wife MARY OGSTON d.19 Oct.1964 aged 79.

---

336 In loving memory of JOHN ROGIE farmer Netherton d.23 Apr.1975 aged 71. Dear husband & father.

---

337 Sacred to the memory of BARBARA SIM b.9 Sept.1872 - d.13 Jan.1955. Her brother CHARLES WILLIAM SIM b.7 May 1877 - d.10 Dec.1958 of Cuttieshillock, Coull.

---

338 In loving memory of WALTER DALGLEISH d.9 Apr.1955. His wife ROBERTA FRASER d.11 Mar.1982.

---

339   In loving memory of ELIZABETH KEIL d.Braes Manse, Logie Coldstone, Dinnet 3 May 1958 beloved wife of LEWIS FORBES late of Tillykerrie Farm. Above LEWIS FORBES d.Braes Manse, Logie Coldstone, Dinnet 9 May 1968.

----

340   (Shield -facing other way) In loving memory of WILLIAM H. ESSON d.9 June 1941 aged 54. From his wife, Rowanbank, Tarland.

----

341   In loving memory of FRANCIS W.RAMSAY d.14 July 1956 beloved husband of CAROLINE E.S.WEBSTER d.6 Jan.1982.

WAR MEMORIAL
Situated at the West end of the main square of the village.

In grateful remembrance
of men of this Parish who gave their lives
for their King and Country
in the Great War.
1914 - 1918

Cpl. ROBERT BAPTIE 8 Gord.Hghrs
Gnr. DOUGLAS CAMERON R.G.A.
Pte. JOHN COUTTS 1/7 Gord.Hghrs
  "   JAMES CRAWFORD 1/7 Gord.Hghrs
  "   ALEXANDER CRUICKSHANK 1/7 Gord.Hhrs
  "   ALEXANDER DOW 1/7 Gord.Hghrs
  "   GEORGE S.J.EWEN 1/7 Gord.Hghrs
  "   JAMES H.FERRIES M.G.C.
  "   ROBERT GRANT 1/7 Gord.Hghrs

  "   JAMES GLASS 1/7 Gord.Hghrs

  "   SAMUEL MASSON R.A.S.C.
  "   JOHN MIDDLETON 1/7 Gord.Hghrs
  "   WILLIAM MIDDLETON 1/7 Gord.Hghrs
  "   ALEXANDER MORRISON 1/7 Gord.Hghrs
  "   GEORGE MUNRO 1/7 Gord.Hghrs
  "   WILLIAM MUNRO 1/7 Gord.Hghrs
  "   CHARLES R.PEAT Aus.Imp.Force
  "   JAMES ROSS Royal Scots
  "   WILLIAM ROSS 1/7 Gord.Hghrs
  "   ALLAN M.WALKER 1/7 Gord.Hghrs
Gnr CHARLES R.WALKER R.G.A.
Pte. ALEX.CRAWFORD R.A.S.C.
  "   LEWIS G.McKENZIE 1/5 Gord.Hghrs
  "   MALCOLM N.SMITH 1/6 Gord.Hghrs
"Their names liveth for evermore"

1939 - 45

A.B. HECTOR M.COUTTS R.N.P.S.
Sgmn.LAWRENCE A.DAVIE R.C.S.
Bds. HECTOR LOVIE 1 Gord.Hghrs
Flt/Lt.Sir RODERICK A.MacROBERT R.A.F.
P/O Sir IAIN W.MacROBERT R.A.F.V.R.
Tpr. ALASTAIR McKENZIE Rhodesian A.C.R.
  "   JOHN MASSON R.T.R.
Sgt. ALEXANDER J.TAYLOR R.A.F.

INDEX

Adam:- 108,276.
Adams:- 155.
Alexander:- 56.
Allan:- 41.
Anderson:- 4,64,65,104,160,165,166,
    167,169,273,287,291,320,
    321,335.
Angus:- 92.
Archibald:- 25,249,270.
Archie:- 117.
Aulay:- 2.
Austin:- 239.

Bain:- 49,226.
Baird:- 331.
Baptie:- 77,WM.
Barrack:- 66.
Barron:- 235.
Bass:- 311.
Begg:- 74,246,334.
Benson:- 179.
Bertram:- 13.
Beveridge:- 76.
Beverly:- 40.
Bey:- 53,99.
Birnie:- 162,267.
Birss:- 72,73,229.
Blackhall:- 308.
Bookless:- 77,78.
Boyd:- 43.
Brebner:- 34,101,107,108,109.
Bremner:- 169,298.
Brock:- 80.
Brown:- 29,60,130.
Bruce:- 26,218,247,285.
Burnett:- 257.

Calder:- 49,88,192,259,283,324.
Cameron:- 24,37,163,WM.
Campbell:- 33.
Catanach:- 43.
Cheyne:- 87.
Clark:- 83,137,138,141,142,143,144,
    145,162,163,169,176,177.
Collie:- 103.
Cooper:- 139,317,330.
Copland:- 151,178,182.
Cowell:- 304.

Coutts:- 8,9,75,76,97,128,164,165,166,167
    168,172,224,225,281282,308,325,
    332,WM.
Craib:- 40.
Craik:- 130.
Cran:- 13,281.
Crawford:- 38,39,203,303,WM.
Cromar:- 65,203,242,294,321.
Cruickshank:- 15,119,WM.
Cryle:- 254.
Cumming:- 128,172,184,221

Dalgleish:- 338.
Daniel:- 14.
Davidson:- 29,89,122,170,192.
Davie:- 208,WM.
Dawson:- 15.
Dewar:- 4.
Dickson:- 208.
Donal:- 230.
Donaldson:- 202,226.
Douglass:- 12.
Dow:- WM.
Duguid:- 256,261.
Duncan:- 59,138,193.
Dunn:- 52.

Easson:- 70.
Ellis:- 16,294,331.
Emslie:- 1,2,229,267.
Erskine:- 13.
Esson:- 36,60,61,63,65,66,67,68,69,70,
    71,72,244,284,340.
Ewen:- 25,93,94,213,214,215,216,289,WM.

Falconer:- 146.
Farquhar:- 37,140.
Farquharson:- 5,11,83,159,210,280,318,323.
Ferres:- 57,58.
Ferries:- 117,214,WM.
Findlay:- 124,268.
Florence:- 238.
Forbes:- 21,35,47,50,69,81,82,83,84,85,
    92,98,108,114,115,161,225,232,
    242,245,262,271,333,339.
Fordyce:- 186.
Forgie:- 333
Forrest:- 120.

ABERDEEN & NORTH-EAST SCOTLAND
FAMILY HISTORY SOCIETY
164 KING STREET
ABERDEEN • SCOTLAND • AB24 5BD

Tel: 01224 - 646323
Fax: 01224 - 639096

www.anesfhs.org.uk

ISBN 1-900173-71-9

£2·99

9 781900 173711 >

AA187

Henry Tren

the Cornish invent
rocket life-saving apparatus

Richard and Bridget Larn

First published in 2006 by Truran,
Croft Prince, Mount Hawke, Truro, Cornwall TR4 8EE

www.truranbooks.co.uk

Truran is an imprint of Truran Books Ltd

Designed by Alix Wood, Bodmin

ISBN–10 1 85022 202 9
ISBN–13 978 185022 202 6

COVER: **Painting by Clive Carter © 2006 – showing the simplicity and lightweight nature of Henry Trengrouse's rocket lifesaving apparatus**

HALF TITLE PAGE: **Portrait of Henry Trengrouse painted when he was 55 years old** (Helston Museum)

Printed in Cornwall by R Booth Ltd, Antron Hill, Mabe, Penryn, TR10 9HH

Henry Trengrouse

the Cornish inventor of the rocket life-saving apparatus

Richard and Bridget Larn

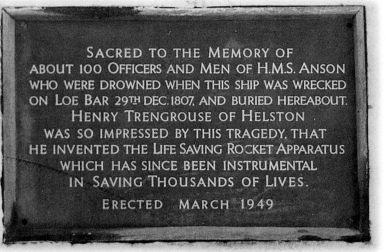

SACRED TO THE MEMORY OF
ABOUT 100 OFFICERS AND MEN OF H.M.S. ANSON
WHO WERE DROWNED WHEN THIS SHIP WAS WRECKED
ON LOE BAR 29TH DEC. 1807, AND BURIED HEREABOUT.
HENRY TRENGROUSE OF HELSTON
WAS SO IMPRESSED BY THIS TRAGEDY, THAT
HE INVENTED THE LIFE SAVING ROCKET APPARATUS
WHICH HAS SINCE BEEN INSTRUMENTAL
IN SAVING THOUSANDS OF LIVES.

ERECTED MARCH 1949

Introduction

THE DEVELOPMENT AND perfection of a means whereby a line could be passed from the shore to an offshore shipwreck or vice versa to save lives, has a long and torturous history, involving numerous inventors over at least seventy years. That Henry Trengrouse of Helston was the inventor of a rocket life-saving apparatus is indisputable, however there were earlier contenders, one of whom patented the idea. Trengrouse was totally unaware of competition when he embarked on his life-long mission, and as a result never received the acclaim, recognition, support or financial reward he truly deserved. He expended a personal fortune on his invention, almost to bankruptcy, to the detriment of himself and his family. His feelings of frustration and despair are revealed in one of his many letters when he wrote:

> *Hope deferred maketh the heart sick. I have experienced the most painful disappointments as well as been at a very heavy expenditure.*

It was a remarkable coincidence that two men who never met, living at opposite ends of the country, witnessed different and tragic shipwrecks involving heavy loss of life in the same year, which completely changed their lives. A Captain Manby watched from the beach at Gt Yarmouth, Norfolk, the death of 50 crew of a Royal Navy brig lost in February 1807, whilst Henry Trengrouse saw over 100 sailors drown that December from a frigate off Porthleven, Cornwall. The wrecks had a profound effect on both men, and although neither were seamen nor professionally associated with the sea, they devoted the rest of their lives to the development of line communication with stranded ships, which would allow passengers and crew to be brought safely ashore.

Unfortunately, John Dennett, an inventor on the Isle of Wight, was already well on the road to achieving a similar goal, and the outcome makes for a fascinating and important account of one of Cornwall's most famous but neglected worthies.

Crew being rescued by breeches-buoy (*Illustrated London News*)

Henry Trengrouse
and the wreck of HMS *Anson*

1807 WAS A YEAR that completely changed the lives of two men, Henry Trengrouse of Helston, Cornwall, and army Captain Edward Manby, of Gt Yarmouth Norfolk, who lived some 370 miles apart and as far as is known neither corresponded nor actually met one another. Both were so affected by shipwrecks they witnessed in 1807, that they devoted the rest of their lives to inventing a means of passing a line by gun or rocket from ship-to-shore, or vice versa, to save lives. It was a remarkable coincidence that both wrecks were Royal Navy men o'war, and were lost in the same year. Both men virtually bankrupted themselves in their pursuit, neither received the official recognition they deserved, and both died bitter, disillusioned and much the poorer in the same year.

That Henry Trengrouse invented a rocket life-saving apparatus is an indisputable fact, and the survival of two complete sets of his equipment, with firing muskets, original rockets and accoutrements in wooden chests in Helston Museum, bear witness to his ingenuity. There is little surviving evidence of Manby's mortar equipment and even less of earlier inventors in this field which include John Dennett, Sir William Congreve; Lieutenant Bell, Colonel Boxer, AG Carte and others. The development of the Rocket Life-Saving Apparatus in the 19th century, usually abbreviated simply to the 'breeches-buoy', which saved countless lives until superseded by Search and Rescue helicopters, has a long, torturous and confusing chronology with numerous claims and counter-claims. It is therefore appropriate to say that no one individual invented this apparatus, but that the final and successful result was a combination of numerous ideas and inventions, plus the total dedication and sincerity of men such as Henry Trengrouse.

Trengrouse was born on 18 March 1772 at Priske Farm, near Mullion, Cornwall; his parents were Nicholas and Mary (née Williams). On completing his education at the local grammar school, Henry served his apprenticeship as a carpenter and cabinet maker, then worked for his father in the trade for a few years before going out on his own, as far a field as London. On 19 November 1795 he returned to Cornwall to marry Mary Jenken of St Erth who bore nine children between 1796 and 1814, four boys and five girls, of whom three died early, Mary and Henry in infancy and another Henry at the age of ten.

Priske Farmhouse, off Polhorman Lane, Mullion, where Henry Trengrouse was born, the family having lived there since the early 1600s *(Richard Larn)*

It was Tuesday, 29th December 1807 when Henry, now aged 32, heard news whilst in his workshop alongside 122 Meneage Street, Helston, that a large ship was embayed off Porthleven and would be wrecked on Loe Bar. It was unlikely this was Henry's first shipwreck, having been born and brought up on the Lizard peninsular, where shipwrecks were commonplace. The family had lived at Priske with its 100 acres since 1655, and only moved to Helston in 1783 to be nearer the Grammar School that Henry was to attend. From that year until he was forced to sell Priske sometime in the 1840s to help finance his invention, the farm was leased to tenants. All the Trengrouse males would have been familiar with the winding coastal footpaths along high cliffs leading to hidden coves that make up this part of Mount's Bay. This included Mullion, Poldhu, Gunwalloe, Dollar Cove, Halzepheron and finally the mile-long Loe Bar leading to Porthleven. As to shipwrecks, most local houses and barns including Priske had overhead beams which carried the adze marks of long-forgotten shipwrights, as well as treenails or copper fasteners, poignant reminders of some long-forgotten wreck whose timbers had been put to good alternative use.

The wreck of HM frigate *Anson* on Loe Bar, Porthleven, Cornwall on 29 December 1807 *(Painting in Helston Museum, by Clive Carter, 1966)*

Trengrouse made his way the three miles to Porthleven on foot, turning off east near Penrose Manor, then over the coast path and down to sea level where a huge shingle bar separates Loe Pool and Helston from the open sea. By the time he arrived, the 44-gun frigate *Anson*, which had been enforcing a blockade of the French port of Brest had become embayed, now lay stranded in the shallows. She was no ordinary frigate having been built at Plymouth in 1781 as a larger 64-gun, 3rd rate man o'war, cut down in 1794 to only 44 guns having proven top heavy and a bad sailer. The *Anson* now lay beam on to a lee shore only 100 yards out, her bow to the east, hard and fast in the shallows, her port side facing the beach with huge seas breaking over the entire ship, the weight of which were slowly tearing her to pieces. When Trengrouse arrived all three masts were still standing, only a tattered remnant of topsail canvas clinging to the foremast, then as he watched her mainmast slowly collapsed to leeward. It came down with an almighty crash, taking with it a great tangle of yards, sails, shrouds, rigging and at least fifty men who had sought its shelter, only to be catapulted into the breakers where most drowned.

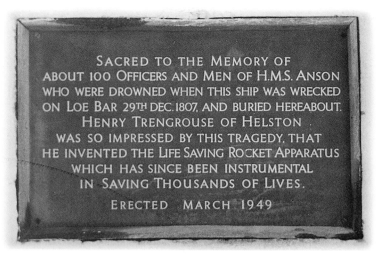

Dedication plaque on the *Anson* Memorial overlooking Loe Bar and the wreck site *(Richard Larn)*

The *Anson* Memorial on the cliffs overlooking Loe Bar and the place where it was wrecked; erected by Councillor Frank Strike of Porthleven, at his personal expense in March 1949 *(Richard Larn)*

CAPT^N CHARLES LYDIARD, R.N.

VIRTUTE ET PRUDENTIA

Captain Charles Lydiard, RN, commander of the Royal Navy frigate *Anson*
who drowned in the wreck on Loe Bar, sacrificing his life to save members of
his crew

(Engraving by J. Gold, 1808, Shoe Lane, London)

Captain Charles Lydiard, Royal Navy, did his utmost to save his crew comprising over 150 men, two women and two children. Stationing himself on the quarterdeck alongside the ship's wheel, he encouraged them to use the fallen mainmast as a bridge to reach the shore. By this means over forty were saved, many assisted by local men who plunged into the breakers with rope around their waists, holding survivors steady against receding waves which otherwise would have swept their feet from under them. A Methodist preacher risked his life to get on board, followed by two other locals who found both women, the children and several men below decks, helping them over the ship's side onto the main mast, towards safety. Unfortunately, both children were swept away and drowned, as was an eleven-year-old ship's boy being assisted by the captain, until they too were caught by a huge wave and dragged into the sea.

An article printed in the *Cornish Telegraph* newspaper in November 1905, credits Henry Trengrouse with having swum out to the wreck and saved the life of a child, also a man knocked over in the shallows that would have drowned had he not grabbed his collar and dragged him to safety. Tobias Roberts and William Foxwell of Helston later received medals from the Humane Society and the Navy Board, accompanied by a letter of thanks for saving lives from the *Anson*. Lesser awards went to William Richards, Charles Courtis and John Triggs of Mullion, Peter Hendy, William Hendy, John Lukey and Renatus Triggs of Gunwalloe, Henry Triggs of Porthleven and Henry Prideaux, of Sithney; but there was no mention of Trengrouse suggesting that there were some unsung heroes that day. Henry remained on the beach until dusk, appalled at the sight of forty or so corpses washing to and fro in the shallows which were later dragged up the pebbly beach then buried in a common unmarked grave on the cliff top.

He arrived home in Helston long after dark, cold, soaked to the skin, exhausted, hungry and very depressed, developing a chill as a result of exposure. His own words record:

At this wreck I got very wet; from the effects of which, and from the cold wind and fatigue, I became much indisposed for several days, and was partially confined to my bed.

During recovery his mind was in torment; how could so many lives be lost so close to the shore; what could be done to prevent a re-occurrence? His account of the wreck continues:

Iron 32-pounder cannon recovered from the wreck of HM frigate *Anson* by
Captain Anderson (centre) of the Western Marine Salvage Company,
Penzance, about 1925; now on display mounted on Porthleven harbour quay
(Gibsons of Scilly)

*It was then and there that the annihilation of this fine ship and so many of my fellow
creatures, most seriously arrested my reflections and sympathy, and freshened in my
memory the primitive destruction of about fifty fine fellows and soldiers at the wreck of
the transport vessel* James & Rebecca.
(nb: less than two miles from the *Anson,* three weeks earlier).

The transfer of a line from ship-to-shore seemed to Trengrouse the obvious
solution, but how best could this be achieved? He found his answer the
following year whilst watching a firework display commemorating
King George III's birthday, with his family. If a thin line could be attached to a
rocket accurately fired towards the coast, could not a stronger rope follow to
create a 'bridge' between ship and shore? If some sort of suspended cradle were
then hung on the 'bridge' a man sitting inside could pull himself to safety,
attached lines allowing the empty cradle to be pulled back to the ship to be used
over and over again until all were saved.

His solution as to how a rocket could be aimed and fired was brilliant, innovative and simple. He designed tin plate half-cylinders either 15in (0.4m) long (large), or 13in (0.3m) (small) with an attachment that fitted over the muzzle of a musket, holding it steady. The body of the rocket sat inside the half-cylinder, its 3ft 6in (1.00m) long stick lying alongside the barrel of the weapon. When a blank charge of gunpowder was fired, *the quantity of powder put into the gun must not exceed a woman's middle size thimble-full.*

The flame passed up the barrel, igniting a short length of 'quick-match' at the base of the rocket. This in turn ignited the rocket compound, causing it to be propelled high into the air, trailing a thin line. Only two operators were required, one to load, aim and fire the musket, the other to hold a simple tapered wooden cone, on which was wound 200 yards (183m) of a thin but strong mackerel line attached to the rocket stick. By night the track of the rocket left a fiery trail giving the operator an idea of the affect of wind and drift should the rocket miss its target, whilst in daylight it left a smoke trail serving the same purpose. The tapered cone pre-wound with line was designed to ensure it ran out smoothly without tangles or knots, but was not always successful. It was later changed for a line 'faked' out in layers in a wooden box. From correspondence we know that Trengrouse ordered muskets and powder flasks from a Mr J B Toulmin of Birmingham, (3 x best guns with twisted barrels of steel, with silver nose caps, £12/12/0, 6 x powder flasks 14 shillings, according to an early invoice), whilst the rockets came from a Mrs Field, a London manufacturer.

As a cabinetmaker, Trengrouse housed his apparatus in special American pine chests, carefully made with dovetail joints, a close fitting lid, and compartments to hold all the accoutrements, including the musket. Fitted with rope handles and a brass lock, each chest measuring 4ft.3in (1.3m) long and 1ft.6in square (0.5m), weighed less than 110lb (50kg), hence easily carried by two men, whether between decks on a ship, or along narrow coastal footpaths. The cost of an apparatus was initially £12, later increased to £20. The argument as to whether this was a 'ship-to-shore' or 'shore-to-ship' equipment was later discussed at great length, but Trengrouse fervently believed it should be the former. If so then every type of vessel afloat could carry one, including lifeboats, pilot boats and revenue cutters, which was Trengrouse's burning ambition, since this could only lead to recognition and orders for countless numbers of sets, but if shore-to-ship, a few dozen at most. His argument in favour of 'ship-to-shore' was that if a ship were stranded then invariably the wind would be blowing towards the coast, hence assisting a rocket in its flight, whereas if

A print of HM *Anson* published many years after the event; note the lines to the vessel and the rocket being fired to the shore. Had this really happened many more would have been saved.

(T Gillard, The Strand, London, 1833)

'shore-to-ship' the rocket would be fired against the wind, greatly reducing its effective distance and accuracy. Similarly, two ships at sea far from land, one sinking; by lying upwind the rescuer could use the apparatus in open water to save lives. Also, a ship presented a relatively small target for a rocket fired from land, whilst the coast offered a huge target for a rocket fired from sea, but a counter argument asked the pertinent question, would people ashore be around to know about a wreck at night, or where rocket lines fell?

We know that Henry Trengrouse was initially unaware of other developments in the field of rocket apparatus when he embarked on his long and costly invention. This was probably due to his isolation by living in Cornwall and lack of contact with current military and maritime affairs. By the end of 1808 he felt he was ready to publicise his invention, and after writing to appropriate authorities and individuals in London making appointments, he set off for the capital on board a small coaster out of Falmouth. He was ebullient, buoyant, confident and totally convinced he would be received with open arms, credited with an invention that would greatly benefit the seafaring community and mankind in general, would save many lives, fulfil his dream, and hopefully make his fortune.

Captain Manby and the wreck of HMS *Snipe*

By comparison with Henry Trengrouse, George Manby had a privileged upbringing, but was described by friends as:

his own worst enemy, something of a genius, a bit of a lunatic, who nobody took very seriously!

He was born at Denver Hall, Norfolk, on 28 November 1765, had a good private education after which his father, an army officer, encouraged him to join the Cambridge Militia but he remained with them only a short period, leaving to marry a Jane Preston, said to be an outstanding beauty. It was an unfortunate marriage since within five years of his father's death, when Manby had inherited Denver Hall and a small fortune, he and Jane had squandered the lot. They moved to Wales, where Jane had an affair with a Captain Pogson; and when Edward found out, during either an argument or a duel Manby was shot in the back of the head. He survived the operation to remove the ball and fragments of a cloth hat he was wearing, but close friends commented that he was never the same again.

Owing large sums his creditors had him arrested for debt but his brother, the commander of a naval frigate, arranged for his release and appointed him of all things his chaplain, in order to get him out of the country. The ship was nearly lost when it ran ashore, and Manby's first hand experience of near shipwreck brought a premature end to his brief seagoing career. Now aged 35, Manby desperately sought means of fame and fortune, even approaching the government offering to go to France and assassinate Emperor Napoleon, an offer that was discretely declined! Impressed by his patriotism, he was appointed barrack master of the military barracks at Gt Yarmouth and given the rank of lieutenant-captain, with quarters in the naval hospital, from where he witnessed the shipwreck that was to change his life.

On 11 February 1807, HM gun brig *Snipe*, commanded by Lieutenant Champion RN, was returning to the Nore at Chatham with French prisoners-of-war from enemy ships taken as prize. Caught by a severe gale off the Norfolk coast she was forced ashore on the sandy beach north of Haven's Mouth, the entrance to Gt Yarmouth's harbour. Manby stood aghast as he witnessed the slow disintegration of the warship less than 50 yards offshore. Despite a freezing gale, driving sleet and rain, he remained on the beach until dusk,

George William Manby Esq.
Engraved for the European Magazine by T. Blood
from an Original Painting by S. Lane.

Portrait of Captain Manby, c1834
(Science Museum Pictorial)

helping to save lives and watched helpless as some 60 drowned, including 30 French prisoners, and a number of women and crew. The frustration of not being able to get a rope out to the ship, or the ship to get a rope ashore struck Manby as ridiculous, and he was equally determined to find a solution.

His military connections gave him access to weapons and powder, and deciding that the solution to the problem lay in the use of a gun, he settled initially on a 24lb (11kg) brass mortar whose weight made it reasonably portable. Early experiments in 1807 failed when either the line attached to the shot broke on firing, or else the powder charge set fire to the line. A chain connection proved too heavy and fireproofing the line with chemicals proved unreliable, so Manby finally settled on a length of wet plaited leather. In a later comparison between the portability of a mortar and a rocket apparatus, a 5½in (14cm) brass mortar weighed 140lb (64kg); its mounting bed and fittings 168lb (76kg); 6 shot of 24lb (11kg) and lines, a further 288lb (131kg), which with cartridges, primers and tools totalled 596lb (270kg). This was a difficult weight to man-handle along cliff paths, over rocks or uneven ground often at night and usually in bad weather. By contrast, six 9lb (4kg) rockets, musket, cartouche, frame, lines and priming tubes weighed only 129lbs (59kg).

Captain Manby's brass mortar which fired the first lifeline from Yarmouth beach around 1807 *(Courtesy of King's Lynn Museums)*

The first use of Manby's mortar apparatus was almost exactly a year after he applied himself to the problems of passing a line to shipwrecks. On 18 February 1808 the Plymouth brig *Elizabeth*, went ashore on the beach at Gt Yarmouth 150 yards (137m) out, and with waves going completely over the deck. Her seven crew took to the rigging to await rescue. Several beach boats were launched but were flung back ashore, so Manby set up his mortar apparatus and the very first shot dropped a line right across the ship, by which means an empty boat was pulled out from the shore. This returned with all the crew, a landmark rescue for which the Suffolk Humane Society awarded him a silver medal.

Encouraged by its first use, Manby improved his apparatus. He invented a 'star shot' that would illuminate a wreck, then a canvas sling hung from special pulleys, by which people could be pulled through breakers to the shore on a floating mattress cum boat. He went on to suggest to Trinity House that to assist identification lighthouses should have a unique and distinctive flashing pattern, and not all flash the same as was current practice, an idea immediately adopted and eminently sensible. It has been said Manby did all this at his own expense but that is most unlikely. In charge of a military depot he had access to all the necessary materials, as well as skilled tradesmen and artisans to carry out most of the work. Manby then took his apparatus to London, set it up in Hyde Park and gave demonstrations before admiring crowds. Support from MPs led to a Parliamentary Committee to consider his invention, and Manby received the recognition he craved, plus an award of £2,000, the equivalent of some £200,000 today. The same committee recommended he be employed to survey the entire coast of Gt Britain, selecting suitable sites for his apparatus. This took two whole years, a most enjoyable commission no doubt, but on completion the government allocated insufficient funds, and initially only Norfolk and Suffolk coastguard stations were given the mortar apparatus.

To his credit Manby worked on several other inventions, a pressurised fire extinguisher, a rescue sledge for use on ice, a sectional ladder buoyed to save skaters who fell through thin ice, and a whaling harpoon gun. His estranged wife died in 1814, and Manby now aged 49, married a wealthy baronet's daughter, Sophia Gooch. She was the complete opposite of his first wife, quiet, submissive, economic and supportive of his activities. They lived in a big house in St Nicholas Road, Gt Yarmouth, within sight of Nelson's seafront monument, which was probably no coincidence since Edward had an obsession concerning the admiral. In 1817 the couple, too old to have children of their own, adopted two brothers, John and William Joy, aged eleven and fourteen, sons of a

Captain Manby's invention to throw a rope to a ship wrecked near the shore
(Science Museum Pictorial)

Yarmouth coachman, who encouraged by their foster parents became accomplished marine artists, whose work is recognised to this day.

Although some mortars were issued to coastguard stations in 1819, they were never widely distributed, official tests later proving them inferior to rockets. Manby's finances despite having a wealthy wife saw him in debt again, and in 1821 it was again expedient for him to leave the country. His whaling harpoon invention was the perfect excuse and he took himself off to sea for one voyage, his name appearing in the crew list of the whaling ship *Baffin* out of Liverpool that year. On his return he went to France at the invitation of Prince de Conde, a relative of his wife, Manby expecting at least a Legion d'Honneur for his work but was disappointed. He spent his life seeking the wealth and honours he felt his inventions deserved but was denied by his importunities.

He was dismissed as master of the Yarmouth barracks in 1845 at the age of 79, still canvassing for recognition, claiming that he had been promised a knighthood, which never materialised, his behaviour becoming more and more erratic. He and his wife retired to a villa on the outskirts of Yarmouth and after she died, Manby took to living in the basement, turning the rest of the house into a quasi Nelson museum, open to the public, which was filled with artefacts and memorabilia relating to the famous admiral. His museum was not the success he had hoped for, few visited, and with no offers to buy the collection, he donated it to the King's Lynn Museum. Manby's obsession with Nelson stemmed from a claim they were great friends from schooldays at Downham Market. Manby went there aged five, but Nelson was seven years older so there was too big an age gap for real friendship, and in fact they were never at school together. Nelson followed his two brothers to the Royal Grammar School at Norwich, then on to Paston School at North Walsham, going to sea with the Royal Navy at the age of twelve; hence Manby's 'friendship' was a delusion. Manby died alone in his basement, aged 89 in 1854, destitute, bitter, unrecognised and forgotten.

—

London and a rude awakening

But for a letter written by his father Nicholas at Helston to Henry Trengrouse, dated 18 November 1800 whilst in lodgings at 3 Bird St, Manchester Square (near Paddington), London, we would be unaware Henry had actually worked in the capital. This explains his intimacy with London and the friends and associates he made who helped him when he returned to publicise and later demonstrate his apparatus. He was 28 when his father wrote to him from home:

Your letter made my heart flow with gratitude to God. Gratefulness to his father for looking after his family. *Young Henry is one of the finest boys of his age in Helston and often comes to his grandfather to shake hands and seems very well. He walks like a*

Mary Trengrouse (née Jenkin), Henry Trengrouse's wife. It is presumed that her portrait was painted at about the same time as her husband's in 1827
(Helston Museum)

lusty fellow and gets over the steps from the kitchen into the Parlour without help. Your wife seems in a very good state of health. We are raising copper ore very fast and have nearly paid our debts on the mine (Gt. Works); expect a dividend about March 1801. Does not want to be paid for looking after family. Wishes Henry to return home soon.

The family to which the letter referred was Henry's wife Mary (née Jenken) who was only nine days older than her husband, and their then two children, Jane (b1796) and Henry (b1799). Their son Henry referred to in the letter died in 1809, aged 10, cause unknown.

Following the wreck of the *Anson* and determined to find a solution to the saving of life from shipwreck, Henry perfected an idea within three months, but had not as yet built any sort of apparatus. He set off for London in March 1808 confident he could sell his invention to the government. What that visit achieved is uncertain since only one relevant letter survives, but from it we can deduce that Henry got nowhere with the authorities.

Dated 17 March 1808 addressed to Croker, secretary at the Admiralty, the letter reveals Trengrouse's feelings, and it is obvious that Henry was ignorant of similar developments regarding rescue apparatus, even that of Captain Manby, already being considered by the government. The suggestion that his idea was not original was a blow to his integrity and pride, since his motives were purely philanthropic, intent only on offering the nation a means of saving countless lives at very little expense:

When I left Cornwall (being well assured of the efficacy attached to my apparatus and plan), I was disposed to flatter myself with what a hearty welcome I should be received and with what gratitude every charitable and Christian mind would hail the day that should usher into the world a production so highly calculated to materially lessen a monstrous evil and to diffuse blessings to mankind. I was aware of the probability that I should encounter difficulties and to overcome and remove obstacles, because instances have rarely occurred of anything new being brought forward to public notice but some have been ready to find fault, to disparage and to oppose. **I was unconscious of any reason existing for the originality of my apparatus to be questioned***.*

I lament that it is questioned at all, the more regret it should be by one of Sir William Congreve's rank and public situation. I regret Sir W.C. should be the person to make this unprovoked attack as being **the original inventor***, that he made such an assertion, because it cannot be substantiated, not by all sophistry in the world. It is probable Sir*

One of two original Trengrouse rocket apparatus chests on display in Helston Museum. The lid held the rockets of different sizes and hence range, held in place by hinged panels. The lower part held all the fittings, rocket lines and the musket *(Helston Museum)*

W.C. has not read my pamphlet, or if he has, not attentively. I do not know what the Naval Chronicle letters allude to; I never saw the book in my life. I now affirm that neither book nor man led me to the contrivance of my apparatus – **there cannot be plainer proof that such another apparatus does not exist** *– had it existed, we should have heard of it in the course of so many years, men do not light a candle and put it under a bushel. Of accounts in London's newspapers none have said, this is an old plan. I think it sufficient to say that* **such another apparatus as mine is not in existence***.*

Trengrouse returned to Helston in the spring of 1808 and did not venture back to London until 1818, ten years later, and one wonders why Henry waited so long to prove that his ideas and apparatus really were the best? He seemingly spent most of that time developing and testing his apparatus before making the first set, then giving demonstrations, writing to various authorities, continuing to seek financial support and of course simply earning a living. Some of his experiments involved rockets fired across Porthleven harbour, transporting people back and forth in a flexible seat grandly called his 'Sailor's Chaise' or

'Chaise Volante'. Each person was required to wear a 'Sailor's Spencer', another Trengrouse invention, a tight fitting canvas belt filled with cork, which was in fact the very first lifejacket. The Mayor of Helston and other dignitaries who witnessed these trials were suitably impressed, and encouraged by their comments Henry wrote to the Society for the Encouragement of Arts, Manufacture & Commerce, inviting them to test his apparatus. With time to reflect on the cool reception received in London, Trengrouse continued to seek support evidenced by a letter of 23 August 1815 from Davies Giddy, MP for Tavistock, who advised that he, *was not hopeful of helping him in Parliament.* Henry

SHIPWRECK INVESTIGATED
Just Published – price 2 shillings.

FOR THE CAUSE of the great loss of lives with which it is frequently attended, and a remedy prescribed in a cheap, portable and practical Life Preserving Apparatus, which is calculated for and is necessary to become a part of every ship's equipment. Its efficacy is fully ascertained by demonstrative applica-tion to the cause of a great number of recent shipwrecks, which are also therein narrated, and from which it plainly appears that its use at only eight of them might have been rendered instrumental to have preserved near two thousand human beings. The Narratives are in themselves very interesting, and many of them have never before been published, BY HENRY TRENGROUSE, HELSTON. *Printed and published by J. Trathan, Falmouth, sold by Mrs. Nettleton,* *Plymouth; Mr. Vigurs, bookseller, Penzance and by the author at Helston.*

nb: As the inventor of the Apparatus intends to make experiments at Falmouth on Thursday next (18th inst) and a few days after at Plymouth, he particularly requests those who feel interested in the preservation of their fellow creatures, to an immediate perusal of his publication, and to become witnesses to his experiments.

nb: The original manuscript edition of his booklet has an introduction not included in the printed edition, which reads:

'The Apparatus that I have **after nearly 10 years application** (but not constant) perfected, as I am certain has never before been thought on. I have studied much for portability and simplicity, firing rockets upwards of half a mile.'

then produced a booklet, *Shipwreck Investigated*, a 47-page essay. The *Royal Cornwall Gazette* newspaper of 13 September 1817 carried an advertisement (see page 25).

Few letters cover Henry's visit to London in 1818, but fortunately those that do cover the crucial aspects of his visit. Taking a chest of rocket apparatus with him by sea to London, Henry, now aged 46, arrived in January and took lodgings at 2 Villiers Street, the Strand. He exhibited his equipment to Admiral Charles Rowley the very next day, who was sufficiently impressed to request the complete chest should be taken to the Admiralty for examination. Henry brought a declaration, signed by officers of the Royal Navy residing in the vicinity of Helston, expressing their – *warmest approbation of the invention and praised the zeal and unremitting perseverance with which Henry Trengrouse had for several years devoted his time, property and health to the completion of his inventions and plans.* Praise indeed. This led to a notice that a committee of officers would assemble at Woolwich to inspect Trengrouse's rockets on 28 February. The Admiralty then advised Henry:

> *the said Committee are to examine Sir William Congreve who has stated that your plan is by no means original and to consider the letters in the Naval Chronicle of 1809 and 1810, and report whether in their opinion you can claim the originality of this invention. My Lords have directed me to inform you that until this experiment be made, and the originality of your plan be proved, they must decline ordering any of your apparatus.*

Henry must have derived great satisfaction from this invitation to demonstrate before men of influence, who were also prepared to challenge Sir William Congreve's counter claim to originality. The report concerning Henry's day at Woolwich Arsenal, dated 2 March reads,

> *I have the honour to acquaint you the Committee of Colonels & Field Officers with Rear Admiral Sir Charles Rawley, Captains Ross and Gower, assembled for the purpose of unpacking an apparatus invented by Mr. Trengrouse. HT exhibited his apparatus consisting of a section of a cylinder fitted to the barrel of a musquet. A small (8oz) rocket fired 180yds; a 1lb rocket carried 450yds but the line broke at 150yds owing to a knot in it; a 1lb rocket fired from a wooden frame at elevation 50 degrees ranged 212yds; a 4oz rocket fired 112yds. The Committee are of the opinion that HT's apparatus appears to them to be the best made for gaining communication with a ship or between ships in heavy gales of wind, and that the experiments they witnessed have fully succeeded since **it appears to be the best mode of gaining a communication with**

Ship-owners, Masters of Vessels, Sailors, their
Wives and Families, and all Seafaring
Persons, are desired to

TAKE NOTICE,

THAT the great WASTE of HUMAN LIFE,
both of SAILORS and PASSENGERS, in the recent
Wreck of the

KILLARNEY STEAM-VESSEL

on the Coast of Ireland, on her passage from Cork
to Bristol, has stimulated thus to offer

TRENGROUSE's APPARATUS,

*For the Saving of Lives and Property in cases of General
Shipwreck, at prices so low as admit of no rea-
sonable excuse for any Vessel being
without it.*

It has gained testimonials from the Admiralty,
and other Official Boards, Naval Officers, &c., de-
claring its superiority. A British Admiral says,
" The Inventions of Mr. Trengrouse for *simplicity,
portability,* and *effect.* in saving men's lives out of a
wreck, *exceed every thing* I am acquainted with."

It is efficient to establish a communication between ships at sea, when severity of weather would
preclude all *attempts* to do it by the usual means,
as in the case of the *Erin* steamer, lost in the Bristol Channel. It is equally applicable to be used on
the shore, as on ship-board, to rescue perishing
men, women, and children, from vessels stranded,
&c., as in the more recent melancholy case of the
Killarney. The Apparatus is all conveniently arranged for immediate use, in a small chest, which
one man may carry.

Application to be made to the Inventor, and orders will be executed with dispatch.—Letters per
post, must be post-paid.

Dated Helston, March 6, 1838.

Advertisement from the *Royal Cornwall Gazette* of March
1838 in which Trengrouse is offering sets of his rocket
apparatus for sale locally *(Cornwall Centre – Redruth)*

the shore for saving lives that has been suggested. Mr. Trengrouse having attended and been shown the two Naval Chronicle letters, as well as a rocket intended for the same purpose as his prepared by Sir William Congreve 10 years ago, Mr. Trengrouse **could not claim the originality of the invention submitted by him.** Mr. Trengrouse declared that he commenced his original experiments in 1807 and that he bought rockets in February 1809. Sir W.C's rockets were then fired in the Barrack Field, with the following results:

18 pounder rocket – 1¹/₂ inch rope – angle 35 degrees – distance fired 250 yards.

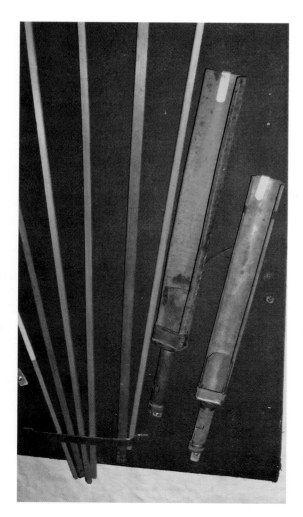

Tinned steel 'open tubes' in two different sizes, which held Trengrouse's rockets when attached to the muzzle of a musket. On firing a blank charge of gunpowder the flash travelled up the gun barrel, through the hollow 'open tube' attachment, setting light to the rockets slow burning composition fuze
(Helston Museum)

10¹/₂-pounder rocket – same rope – 40 degrees – distance 243 yards
9-pounder rocket – same rope – 40 degrees – distance 230 yards.

Still uncertain regarding the originality of Trengrouse's invention, the Commandant at Woolwich Arsenal, Jon Ramsey, wrote him on 24 March following the trial, *Request for more proof of your prior claim.* Having sent it three weeks later, on 11 April Henry received the response he desired:

Concerning Trengrouse's claim to have been first to invent rocket apparatus; **this can be proved** *by letters of 1808 and 1809,* **his claim being fully established. Suggest reimbursing Trengrouse for the expenses he must necessarily have incurred***.*

On 31 May the Admiralty sent the letter he had been waiting for over the past eleven years,

> *Their Lordships are desirous of giving you such encouragement as may afford a fuller and perfected trial of your invention, and therefore desire to know at what price you will supply some of your apparatus for the purpose of being issued to some of His Majesty's ships?*

Henry responded with a price of, £12 per wooden chest set, complete. However, his hopes were dashed on 16 April, when the Admiralty responded:

I am commanded by my Lords Commissioners of the Admiralty to acquaint you, that it had been their intention to purchase Twenty Sets of your Apparatus for preserving lives and property in case of Shipwreck, by way of encouragement, but that the Committee of Naval & Military Officers, who lately witnessed experiments of it, having recommended that the Apparatus should be supplied to His Majesty's ships from the Ordnance Department, rather than by you, and their Lordships being unwilling that you should suffer by this change of determination, they have directed the Navy Board, in lieu of purchasing the said number, to pay you the sum of Fifty Pounds, which their Lordships consider is a very liberal calculation of the profit you might have made in furnishing the Apparatus. I am etc, J. W. Croker.

Attempting to gather further support from Woolwich, Henry wrote the commandant asking for a copy of the minutes of the second trial of his rockets, only to be told that no minutes had been kept, but that *the Committee were satisfied with the experiments.* The House of Commons also ordered that, *all letters relating to Mr. Trengrouse's invention be printed on 7 June 1818 and distributed.*

A most important part of the Trengrouse apparatus was this brass 'double-roller snatch block', which would run along the main hawser carrying survivors; the block having a hinged portion which allowed easy attachment *(Helston Museum)*

A memorandum by Henry dated July 1818 relates to a naval Lieutenant Oke, introduced to him at the Admiralty, who seemingly attempted to steal his invention. Henry, in correspondence, remarked:

In the simplicity of my own heart I showed him my apparatus and explained it throughout, offering to reimburse him if successful in getting the Admiralty to place a firm order. Took gun, rockets and line to Lt Oke for experiments, but Oke's brother presented plans to the Admiralty as his own, suggesting a better chance of success if presented by a naval officer, and a greater reward.

Henry returned to Helston in August, and derived some satisfaction from a report by the Committee of Elder Brethren of Trinity House which stated, *it appears a very probable means of saving lives from vessels driven on shore or stranded.* Henry now seemingly had the support of both the Royal and Merchant Navies, but unfortunately still no orders resulted.

Unwilling to give up, he was back in London in 1819 and whilst there was introduced to the Duke of Kent at Kensington Palace, showing him his apparatus, *which much pleased His Royal Highness.* Better still, Henry arranged a public demonstration on 15 May in Hyde Park, fully reported in the *The Times* and *Morning Post.* Rockets were fired across the Serpentine River into trees, hawsers being set up and men conveyed across as if from a shipwreck. Present

Henry Trengrouse's early 'sailors chasse' or seat, used to transport survivors ashore, eventually replaced by the 'breeches buoy' which held a survivor more securely *(Helston Museum)*

were His Royal Highness, the Swedish Ambassador and the Russian Prince Volkonsky. The latter was so impressed he invited Trengrouse to Russia, presenting him with a valuable gold and diamond ring and £50. In return Henry later sent the prince one of his 'Life Spencers'. Members of the Society of Arts, who, manifested their large approbation of the apparatus by voting him their large gold medal and 50 guineas, also witnessed a demonstration at the same location.

On 4 March 1821 a 100-ton fruit sloop named *Peggy*, Lisbon to London via Fowey with oranges, drove ashore at Porthleven. Assisted by Tobias Roberts, previously awarded a silver medal for his part in both the *James & Rebecca* and *Anson* shipwrecks, Trengrouse collected his apparatus that was stored at Penrose manor, and a line was successfully fired across the wreck. This was the very first occasion that his invention was put to practical use. Unfortunately for Henry the crew elected to remain on board until low tide, when they simply put a ladder over the side and climbed to safety! By way of consolation, the apparatus proved its worth by bringing ashore many boxes of the cargo before the ship finally went to pieces, but no lives were saved.

Trengrouse's journals reveal many interesting aspects of his life and the following shortened version of events cover two separate London visits:

22.5.1825 – *Whitsunday, beautiful day, I rather better than lately. Dined at Morgan's, Covent Garden – 1 shilling. In afternoon to Queen St. chapel; tea at Holborn – 4¹/₂d, coffee at Roberts, home to bed past 9.*

One of Trengrouse's original rocket launching tubes, with rocket fitted ready for firing *(Helston Museum)*

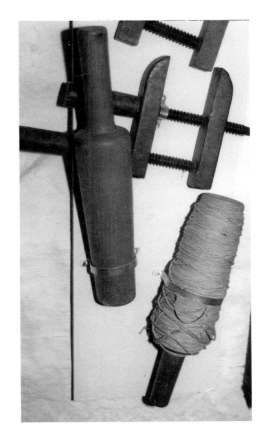

Two tapered wooden 'cones', used to hold the thin line attached to the rocket, allowing the line to easily run off as the projectile passed over a wreck. This was not an ideal solution since Trengrouse frequently experienced problems and 'knotting' of the line; finally settling for a frame holding metal pins which allowed the line to be 'flaked' flat in layers *(Helston Museum)*

23.5 – *Mr Dowson spoke to me, said something must be done about the ring*.

> *Dined at Old Bailey – 9 shillings; at 2 called at Boulay Mews, no Doctor there, sat till 3.30 over wine and water; head not well by this and very dull. Coffee house at St. Martin's Court for tea – 4¹/₂ pence; took tea and loaf near Waterloo Bridge and came home by candlelight.*

HT replied to Dowson: *I wish to retain the ring – have some prospect of redeeming it by Christmas, but more money needed than would be raised by its sale. Do by the ring as seemeth good. I would like the stone to be sold & setting retained – that at a future day I might have it filled with paste in imitation of the real one, to show my family & friends – (my) rich relations do not come to help. My health is not good.*

24.5 – *To Owens, brass worker; traveller not finished; wrote letter and made copy to Mr. Cork. Bread, cheese & beer by the way – 5¹/₄d, home at 11, fine night.*

25.5 – *Went to Dr. Birbeck, presented him with traveller, said he would hang it in Mechanics Institution and invited me there. In Tooley Street met Captain Barne who readily lent me* a sovereign, went with him for some beer.

26.5 – *Went to Counting House at Cotton's Wharf and paid in part of £4 I had on 14th. Over Blackfriars to Copplestones, drank 3 cups of tea – 8d, felt rather a trembling afterwards.*

28.5 – *Saw Sir Ackland, said my apparatus being approved by the Committee should not have been returned. Slept at an inn, awoke about 5 with headache, better after breakfast – 1s.3d; bed – 1s. Coach fare each way – 1s.6d = 3s.*

30.5 – *Sir William Hillary called, looked at apparatus, had seen founder of Shipwreck Institution and thought he ought to be instrumental to bringing my apparatus into use. Thought he should have 4 or 5 Spensers, a chair, travellers, lines and 4 dozen rockets.*

31.5 – *Dined at Whites Lamb Chop House – 1s. Paid Whites for borrowed 5s.0d; called on cousin at Lombard St, paid for borrowed 10s.0d.*

2.6 – *Went to Surrey St, to get address of Admiral Donnely from his agent; felt great lassitude, tea at Copplestones – 6d*

3.6 – *Petition presented this evening, the Committee decided in my favour; saw* The Times, *which was very brief on the subject.*

1.8 – *Went to Deptford. Took 2s. in my pocket thinking that would pay coachman, but he charges more on Sunday so obliged to borrow 1s.*

17.8 – *Mr. Henger & Co. have 2 sets of tools for making 2 sizes large rockets, which belong to me. I took my box with model gig to Dolly Clarks.*

18.8 – *Called at Mr. Huggins, marine painter, talked about a picture of the* Anson. *Boat hire – 1s; biscuits and gin – 6d. Mr. Huggins is a marine painter in Leadenhall St, has my drawings after the wreck of the* Anson, *purposing to do one in time for the exhibition. Paid Mrs. Leopards Coffee House, owing – 6d; rice-pudding on the way home – 2d; 14 eggs at Mr. Greatheads – 1s; paid Williamson for borrowed the 3rd £1, do for a glass of gin - 2¹/2d. Paid Mrs. Cottle my washerwoman on account – 4s; Dorbrees for coat and watch - £3.7s.6d.*

22.8 – *Called at Mrs. Fields, she promised rockets on Thursday.*

23.8 – *Wrote secretary Shipwreck Institution informing my preparing to leave. Wrote Mrs. Price, would she accommodate me with credit for 40 or 50s for 2 months. I intend leaving Saturday, Mr. Dowson wants the money or the ring, must be sold. Told me Mr. Gamon wanted his money; gone to the country and left ring with him. He supposed the ring would not sell for more than would pay Mr. Gamon.*

24.8 – *Letter from Shipwreck Institution to send chest of apparatus to their office, with bill.*

25.8 – *Got to wharf, saw the Mate and agreed to bring my luggage on Monday, said he would sail Tuesday, To Mr. Harris's, Southwark Bridge, had 2 large travellers off him, paid 10s.*

26.8 – *Sir William Hillary called, tarried till 12, striving for Government to compel all vessels to carry apparatus. Asked what it would cost, and I said about £20 to £25; said Committee expected it to exceed that sum, much approved my exertions & hoped I would be remunerated, said* **'The Ministers ought to have settled an annuity on me and my family'.**

A BRIEF DESCRIPTION

OF,

AND DIRECTIONS FOR USING

TRENGROUSE'S APPARATUS

FOR THE

PRESERVATION OF LIVES AND PROPERTY

IN CASES OF

GENERAL SHIPWRECK;

AND

FOR ASSISTING VESSELS IN DISTRESS AT SEA, &c.

With a few cases Demonstrative of its Efficiency.

"I call Mr. Trengrouse THE SAILOR'S FRIEND."

Admiral Sir Charles Rowley.

"The Inventions of Mr. Trengrouse of the west of England, for *Simplicity, Portability,* and *Effect* in saving men's lives out of a wreck, exceed every thing I am acquainted with."

Admiral Spranger's Essay.

LONDON:

PUBLISHED BY J. RICHARDSON, ROYAL EXCHANGE;

And may be had of J. Philp, Printer, Falmouth, and all other Booksellers.

Front page of Trengrouse's pamplet concerning his invention and directions for use in the case of general shipwreck *(Richard Larn)*

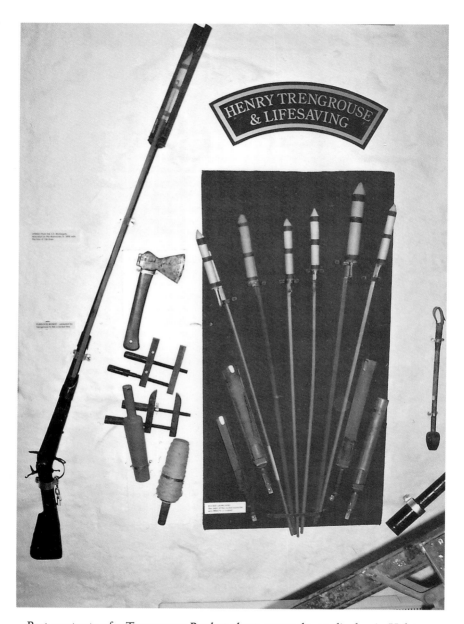

Part contents of a Trengrouse Rocket chest currently on display in Helston Museum. Different sizes of his rockets are shown, four metal rocket launchers, a lead weighted throwing cane, tapered line 'cones' and a musket ready to fire

(Helston Museum)

27.8 – *I unwell. Letter to Mr. Field, rocket maker. Went to Mr. Benny's to ask about sailing of the* Enterprize *(to Falmouth). Felt unwell, took tea in Picket Row – 3d.* Enterprize *will not sail till middle of week. Tincture of myrrh for my teeth, which with no gums were painful. One ounce – 6d.*

30.8 – *Started for boat at Cottons Wharf and put chest on board; but now won't sail before Friday. Paid the waterman – 2s.*

Following 20 years of development Trengrouse was still no nearer making any viable sales of his equipment. Having expended some £3,000 of his own and family money on his invention, plus an additional legacy of £500 from an older brother, one has to ask the question, 'why was his rocket apparatus unacceptable to Government and why did Trengrouse not succeed?'

Seemingly, everyone who witnessed a demonstration of its potential agreed it was an outstanding idea and recommended it, but still neither the Royal Navy nor shipping companies would buy it. Till his dying day Henry advocated that 'ship-to-shore' rescue was preferable to 'shore-to-ship'; even the Committee of Pilotage & Examination in their 1818 report said:

It is highly preferable to any other mode as it will be always ready at hand, and may be easily discovered, even at night by persons on shore, and do therefore recommend that vessels (the cost being so trivial) should never be without the apparatus of the Rocket.

Judging him by his grammar school education, his incredibly neat handwriting, sound command of English in his many letters and meticulous notes made in his journals, Trengrouse appears a self-effacing, reserved, quiet gentleman, who saw himself as a man of science, of whom people took advantage. His isolation of residence in west Cornwall, his lack of influential political or social contact in London, and his failure to patent his apparatus at an early stage, plus a stubborn inflexibility in his insistence that 'ship-to-shore' rescue was the only way forward, all contributed to his failure.

Had he projected himself and his invention earlier instead of wasting ten whole years in dreaming, whilst others forcefully progressed similar ideas, Trengrouse would probably have succeeded. Captain Manby with his military approach to the problem, was an altogether more outgoing character, used to giving orders and being obeyed, did not waste any time with his development, and for an outlay of only £50 of personal money, not only got his mortar apparatus accepted but actually issued to coastguard stations the length of the country. However, mortar apparatus for 'shore-to-ship' communication was soon condemned on safety grounds, several men allegedly having been killed on the deck of ships, struck by what was literally a high velocity iron cannon ball.

The Dutch Ambassador wrote to Trengrouse supporting his invention, as did the Royal Humane Society and Elder Brethren of Trinity House. Other inventors were now suggesting inflated balloons carrying a line would more easily blow ashore, others suggested kites would be preferable, but the government still would have none of it despite an ever-increasing loss of ships and men. Even in the Shipping Protection Bill before Parliament in 1837, the subject of rescue apparatus was neither mentioned nor recommended. Whilst it took time for the authorities to recognise the value of both Trengrouse's and Dennett's rocket apparatus, both consistently outperformed the mortar, and won the day on cost, portability and accuracy. One further drawback for Trengrouse was that Dennett's son went into business with his father manufacturing rocket sets in their Isle of Wight workshop, selling them to government.

Henry never returned to London after 1838, settling down to a sedentary family life in Helston, still corresponding with authorities, relentlessly pursuing his ambition and dream. He continued to live with his wife, children and grand-children in Meneage Street, the 1851 census return showing that there were ten members of the Trengrouse family resident, ranging from a one–year–old to Henry at 79, described as a 'gentleman'. He died on Tuesday 15 February 1854, aged 82, at the family home in Helston. His eldest son Nicholas, now 39 years of age and a successful Helston auctioneer was at his bedside when Henry spoke his last words, 'If you live to be as old as I am, you will find my rocket apparatus all along our shores.' It is said he then turned over to face the wall, and quietly died. His prediction of course came true, his rocket apparatus became accepted internationally, saving countless thousands of lives worldwide.

—

A History of Life-Saving Apparatus

Rockets were no novelty when Trengrouse began his experiments, having been around since the Chinese invented gunpowder in 200BC. Used originally as fireworks, by 1200AD rockets had also developed into weapons of war, carrying both a powerful propulsion charge and explosive or incendiary warheads in metal tubes, whose sole function was to cause death or destruction. Early multiple launchers could hold up to 1,000 'fire-arrows' or 'fire-pots,' capable of setting a whole city on fire as they landed on thatched roofs. Joan of Arc's French army used war rockets in 1429 to defend the city of Orleans; Colonel Friedrich, a German, developed war rockets weighing up to 120lb (54kg) in 1668, and by 1680 Peter the Great had established a Russian rocket factory producing missiles capable of illuminating an entire battlefield at night. In India, rockets were fired from ships at enemy coastlines to start bush fires, sending flames and smoke sweeping through settlements and fortifications. The English word 'rocket' derives from the Italian 'rochetta', which was first used to describe such weapons in 1379. Rockets therefore have a long history of their own, and in addition to signalling distress at sea, their maritime adaptation to line-throwing was a further development of their use.

It was a Colonel (later Sir) William Congreve, who began to study captured Indian war rockets at the Woolwich Arsenal's Royal Laboratory in 1804, and who was later to challenge the originality of Trengrouse's apparatus. Named after their developer, Congreve rockets ranging from 18 to 300lb (8-136kg) weight had been accepted into the British army. His 32lb (14.5kg) rocket was the favoured new battle weapon, its metal casing 104cm long by 10cm diameter, was fitted with 4.5m long wooden stick to stabilise its flight. September 1814 saw a 25-hour barrage fired from HMS *Erebus*, against Fort McHenry at Baltimore, resulting in a number of American ships being set on fire and destroyed. The *Erebus*, technically a 24-gun, sixth rate man o'war, described by the Admiralty as a 'rocket vessel', was fitted with 20 batteries of Congreve rockets, each battery holding multiple metal firing tubes. Francis Scott Key, the lawyer who wrote the US National anthem 'The Star Spangled Banner', mentions Congreve weapons in his song with the words, *rockets' red glare*.

Trengrouse conceived his rocket 'idea' in 1808, but took until 1818 to develop a complete working apparatus. Captain Manby who started in 1807 had meantime finished and demonstrated his mortar equipment, first used in anger to save seven men from a wreck at Gt Yarmouth in February 1808, and by 1814 the government had issued 45 sets of his mortars to coastguard and preventive service stations. Manby's mortar idea may not in fact have been original, since a Lt Bell (1747–1798) of the Royal Artillery, Gt Yarmouth, put forward the idea as early as 1791. When Manby demonstrated his equipment in 1808, the witnessing Committee of Field Officers noted in their minutes, *it is incumbent on them to note the late Lieutenant Bell near 14 years since was presented with a premium of 50 guineas by the Society of Arts for similar ordnance communication, shore to ship.*

Another important contender in the rocket business was John Dennett of Clatterford Road, Carisbrooke, Isle of Wight. Born on 25 September 1780, he was something of an inventor. He was described as an antiquarian having studied naval and military mechanics including war rockets as a hobby. He sought to arm both Royal Navy and British merchant ships with war rockets to supplant guns, since they took up little room allowing the great weight of conventional cannon and shot to be dispensed with, making ships much lighter and requiring less crew. Dennett was also experimenting with a life-saving rocket apparatus, and in trials in January 1826 before a Committee of Naval and Military officers at Portsmouth, they concluded, *it was preferable to every other apparatus they had hitherto seen.* The Royal National Institution for the Preservation of Life from Shipwreck (forerunner of the RNLI) immediately ordered three sets that were placed at the Freshwater, Atherfield and St Lawrence coastguard stations on the Isle of Wight. Another trial conducted at Freshwater Gate on the island on 2 June 1827 before coastguard officers, saw comparative tests carried out of rocket and mortar apparatus, throwing lines between flagstaffs 200 yards (183m) apart. Naval lieutenants present accustomed to seeing the mortar apparatus in use, *were of the opinion that the Rocket Apparatus had most decidedly the advantage of Captain Manby's.*

The ultimate test came five years later on 8 October 1832, when the 430-ton ship *Bainbridge* was wrecked on Atherfield Rocks, on the Isle of Wight, 500 yd (457m) offshore. A Manby mortar was set up at the foot of the cliff but four attempts failed to place a line across the ship, by which time a Dennett rocket apparatus had arrived. Its very first shot dropped a line neatly across the deck, by which means a heavier line allowed a boat to be pulled out from the shore, which in two trips saved all eighteen crew and the one passenger. On 2 February 1833 Dennett applied for a patent to cover his apparatus, entitled *Mortars and War Rockets* but with no reference to life-saving in its title. Six pages of text with illustrations elaborate on these topics, including Dennett's *self-*

Rocket Line carried over Wreck

One of Dennett's rockets taking a line to a wreck.
(Richard Larn)

inflating life-slings, a sort of lifejacket *for conveying people to the shore, more safe and convenient than a cot or any apparatus in present use.* On 25 January 1839, six years later, the Patent was granted when:

> *The aforesaid John Dennett came before our said Lady the Queen in her Chancery, and acknowledged the Specification aforesaid, in form above written.*

Dennett certainly derived considerable financial benefit from his patent, and if only Henry Trengrouse had taken similar action in 1808, ie. 31 years earlier, things might have turned out very differently for the Helston rocket man.

The future queen of England, still Princess Victoria, and the Duchess of Kent actually requested a demonstration of Dennett's rockets which took place at St Lawrence Cottage, near Ventnor, on the Earl of Yarborough's estate, Isle of Wight, on 6 August 1833. By 1853 a rocket life-saving apparatus incorporating the best aspects of both Trengrouse and Dennett's inventions had been adopted around the entire coast, officially supplied to 120 Coastguard Stations, these were almost certainly manufactured by John Dennett and his son Horatio, in their workshop premises in Gunville Lane, Carisbrooke. Later the additional power and range of the Boxer rocket, developed by an American Colonel Boxer became universally accepted, but otherwise the apparatus remained the same.

**A breeches buoy showing the basic cork life-ring to which is attached a pair of
canvas 'trousers' which replaced Trengrouse's 'sailor's spencer'**
(Helston Museum)

There is no known specific date when the Trengrouse/Dennett rocket apparatus was officially accepted, but some sort of official trials commenced in 1835. Comparison training of rocket/mortar was officially given to coastguards at Yarmouth, IOW on 24 January that year, then at Blyth on 20 August, Holy Island on the 25th, at Seahouses on the 26th and Tynemouth on the 29th. In 1839 the rocket apparatus was used at the wreck of the *Prince Regent* in Tramore

Bay, Ireland, but was unable to reach the wreck, so a local man swam out with a line (for which he was awarded a silver medal) saving 40 men, women and children, and a similar apparatus is known to have been kept at Ballymacan, Co Waterford. In 1841 silver medals of the RNLI were awarded to coastguards at Padstow, when rockets saved six men from the brig *Britannia* on 31 March. Three similar awards went to men at Bude in 1845 and 1869, when the schooner *Margaret* and brig *Avonmore* were wrecked, which serves to illustrate its widespread acceptance and use. There is an interesting slant on rescue from shipwreck concerned the brig *Liddell*, ashore on a bank near Happisburgh, Norfolk in December 1841. A rocket line was fired across the ship and not understanding its purpose, the crew attached it to their main anchor hawser and fed several cable lengths of it overboard, thinking that those ashore would use it to pull the entire ship to safety!

In a trade directory of 1859, five years after Trengrouse's death, Horatio Dennett (the son) is described as *a rocket manufacturer* living at 89 Clatterford Road, Isle of Wight, and by 1881 as a *retired manufacturer of Dennett's rockets*. John Dennett died on 10 July 1852 aged 72, two years before Trengrouse and Manby,

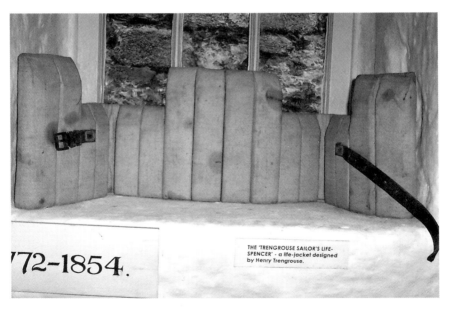

The Trengrouse 'life-spencer', probably the first cork filled life-jacket, later adopted by the RNLI and others *(Helston Museum)*

the son Horatio on 28 November 1897, father and son being buried side-by-side at Carisbrooke church on the island.

Other contributors to the life-saving apparatus were a Frenchman named Le Fere, who in the late 1790s was testing a mortar for life-saving; William Mallison who devised a cork-lifejacket in 1810–11, suggesting that 3lb (1½kg) of cork would support a man afloat; Messrs Mackintosh were marketing a 'Sailors' Swimming Jacket' in 1830, and an Admiral Kisbee invented the ring lifebuoy, to which he later attached a pair of canvas 'breeches' leading to the expression 'breeches-buoy' apparatus, which was shown at the Paris Exhibition of 1854. An obscure participant was Lt Cartes RN, of whom little is known, except that on 20 September 1844, according to the British Association for the Advancement of Science, *there was a very interesting exhibition of experiments with Lieut. Cartes rockets for giving relief to shipwrecked vessels in the grounds behind St. Paul's School at Clifden. A local Society has been the means of placing many of these at different*

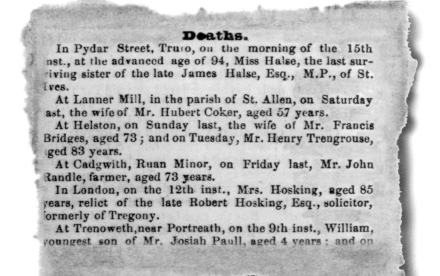

Deaths.

In Pydar Street, Truro, on the morning of the 15th inst., at the advanced age of 94, Miss Halse, the last surviving sister of the late James Halse, Esq., M.P., of St. Ives.

At Lanner Mill, in the parish of St. Allen, on Saturday last, the wife of Mr. Hubert Coker, aged 57 years.

At Helston, on Sunday last, the wife of Mr. Francis Bridges, aged 73 ; and on Tuesday, Mr. Henry Trengrouse, aged 83 years.

At Cadgwith, Ruan Minor, on Friday last, Mr. John Randle, farmer, aged 73 years.

In London, on the 12th inst., Mrs. Hosking, aged 85 years, relict of the late Robert Hosking, Esq., solicitor, formerly of Tregony.

At Trenoweth, near Portreath, on the 9th inst., William, youngest son of Mr. Josiah Paull, aged 4 years ; and on

Death notice for Henry Trengrouse who died aged 83 on Tuesday 15 February 1854. Surprisingly none of the Cornish newspapers printed an obituary
(Royal Cornwall Gazette)

stations on the coast of Yorkshire; Lieut. Cartes also exhibited the effects of his lifebuoy in the neighbouring river.

Somewhere amongst all these equipments was one by Dillon and Rogers whose patented *improved mortar* was demonstrated at about the time the Mercantile Marine Fund finally accepted the cost of establishing rockets around the coast. Despite Henry Trengrouse insisting that rocket apparatus should be ship-borne, it was a vain hope that ship owners were going to buy them and no legislation was forthcoming that might make them compulsory. Had the apparatus been carried on ships there is no argument that many more lives would have been saved, but it was not to be. Sailing ship losses around the UK peaked in 1864 with 1,741 vessels and 516 lives; steamships in 1880, with 1,303 ships and 2,100 lives declining to 733 vessels by 1909 but with 4,738 lives lost, reflecting larger ships carrying more passengers. By comparison, in 2005 there were less than a ten wrecks on our coast and less than 18 lives lost. The last use of a breeches-buoy rocket apparatus is believed to have been on the Isle of Man in July 1981, and on 31 March 1988 it was withdrawn from service throughout the United Kingdom. Search and Rescue helicopters have taken its place, supplemented by part-volunteer coastguard cliff-rescue teams. From the introduction of the Merchant Shipping Act in 1854 and the resultant widespread use of the rocket apparatus pioneered by Henry Trengrouse, Manby and Dennett, it is recorded as having saved over 14,000 lives. Whilst Trengrouse may have died a disillusioned and disappointed man, his work and sacrifice were not in vain.

—

Henry Trengrouse's memorial tomb stone in Helston parish church

The epitaph on Henry Trengrouse's memorial stone:

*ever grateful remembrance of Henry Trengrouse. Of this Borough who, profoundly impressed
by the great loss of life by shipwreck, rendered most signal service to humanity, by devoting the
greater portion of his life and means, to the invention and adoption of the ROCKET APPARATUS,
for communicating between stranded ships and the shore, whereby many thousands of lives
have been saved*

They rest from their labours; and their works do follow them
(Richard Larn)

Acknowledgments

The authors wish to acknowledge the assistance and co-operation given by Martin K Matthews, past curator of Helston Museum, who lives in Henry Trengrouse's old house in Meneage Street (by coincidence both men share the same birthday); also Janet Spargo, the current curator of Helston Museum who allowed us access to their Trengrouse file and gave permission to take and use photographs. Also to the staff of the Cornwall Centre Library, Redruth, and Angela Broome, Librarian of the Royal Institute of Cornwall, Truro; Gail Dodd of Wandi, West Australia; Tim Thorpe, Curator, King's Lynn Museum; Rosemary Cooper, Carisbrooke Castle Museum; Patrick Nott, Carisbrooke, Isle of Wight; and the Norfolk County Records Office, Norwich. Photographic and illustration acknowledgments: Clive Carter, for his specially produced cover painting.

Richard and Bridget Larn

The authors are well qualified to write this definitive mini-biography of Henry Trengrouse, the Cornishman who invented the 'breeches-buoy' rocket apparatus.

Richard and Bridget Larn have published over forty maritime publications and have an international reputation for their books on shipwrecks, diving and maritime history.

Richard lived in Helston for six years, and assisted underwater in the diving operations to recover cannons and artefacts from the wreck of HM frigate *Anson* on Loe Bar, including the huge 32-pounder gun now outside Helston Museum. He designed and created their first exhibition of the Trengrouse rocket apparatus, which is now on permanent display.

The life of Henry Trengrouse, a largely forgotten figure in Cornwall's history, has long been an interest of the authors and this present work is the result of many years' research in the public archives in Cornwall and London, uncovering many aspects of his life, published here for the first time.